T0015185

BRIAN D'AMBROSIO

MONTANA ECCENTRICS

A COLLECTION OF EXTRAORDINARY MONTANANS, PAST AND PRESENT

RIVERBEND
PUBLISHING

RIVERBEND
PUBLISHING

An imprint of Globe Pequot, the trade division of
The Rowman & Littlefield Publishing Group, Inc.

4501 Forbes Blvd., Ste. 200
Lanham, MD 20706

www.rowman.com

Distributed by NATIONAL BOOK NETWORK

Montana Eccentrics

Copyright 2023 © Brian D'Ambrosio

ISBN: 978-1-60639-138-9

Printed in USA

1 2 3 4 5 6 7 8 FS 26 25 24 23 22

All rights reserved. No part of this book may be reproduced, stored, or
transmitted in any form or by any means without the prior permission of the
publisher, except for brief excerpts for reviews.

Cover and text design by Sarah Cauble, www.sarahcauble.com

Front cover photographs, clockwise from top left:
L. Ron Hubbard, Dorothy Johnson, Maria Montana, Reggie Watts,
Sean Kochel, Elizabeth Clare Prophet

ALSO BY BRIAN D'AMBROSIO

Selected Works

From Haikus to Hatmaking:
One Year In the Life of Western Montana

Warrior in the Ring: The Life of Marvin Camel,
American Indian World Champion Boxer

Shot in Montana: A History of Big Sky Cinema

Montana and the NFL

Montana Entertainers, Famous and Almost Forgotten

Montana Murders: Notorious and Unsolved

ACKNOWLEDGMENTS

To all the eccentrics, past and present, who've found a creative
and industrious and positive outlet for their ideas and visions
and strangest charms.

To Violet Mary D'Ambrosio,
with absolute love and eternal memory

CONTENTS

SECTION ONE

A Gallery of Bygone Eccentrics

Section Two

A Gallery of Present-Day Eccentrics

INTRODUCTION

ec•cen•tric

adjective
Departing from a recognized, conventional, or established norm or pattern.

noun
One that deviates markedly from an established norm, especially a person of odd or unconventional behavior.

The American Heritage Dictionary of the English Language

PROPONENTS SPEAK WISTFULLY of that elusive Montana characteristic called "quality of life." Relatively unspoiled space and comparatively few people represent an advantage. On a popular level, this realization evolved into a Montana that offered other Americans a place of protection from urban difficulties, a faddish site for Hollywood stars to regenerate, and a scenic land where one could "return to nature," or perhaps even "discover oneself."

While the land itself is the ultimate natural resource, the rights and will of the individual holds in high prominence. High mountains and prairie lands and emptiness and beauty can be endlessly absorbing. But the character of the residents is an equally valuable treasure. Although the state is comprised of diverse ecosystems, residents do share some common characteristics—or perhaps that was more so the case in previous decades. Still, some understanding of common ground exists and all Montanans know that special "sense of place," for all are personally involved in the landscape.

Though the recent population upheaval and uptick makes it feel as gusty and changeable as the prairie wind, it has long been noted that you can identify a Montanan. And that sense of identity is tied inexorably to the perceived freedom of the land base. The emotional and intellectual autonomy derived from the land is sometimes used to do good—Maurice Hilleman (1919-2005), the Eastern Montana farm boy changed—and saved—the world through medicine—and sometimes for not so good: Elizabeth Clare Prophet (1939-2009), the New Age prophet in Paradise Valley, whose cult of personality and dark moods instilled a dreadful sense of fatalism and paranoid isolationism in her followers.

This book puts forward and exhibits some of those who have lived out, or currently live out, their time in unfamiliar ways. Since the beginning, Montana has sown and nourished eccentricity as a natural resource. From the Miles City poet and cowpuncher D.J. O'Malley (1867-1943) to the dirigible balloonist George Lowry (1886-1965), many Montanans have stretched colorful lives into full enterprises. From frontier preachers such as William Wesley "Brother Van" Van Orsdel (1848-1919), who rode a circuit on horseback and stagecoach, spreading verse and aphorism over tens of thousands of miles, to L. Ron Hubbard (1911-1986), the founder of Scientology, whose ideas were planted in the Flathead Valley and Western Montana, an inexplicably powerful and curious individualism has always been a pivotal trait.

Some of the subjects in this book are figures mined from the quarry of bygone days, while others are alive and immersed and remain reputable stewards of the eccentric resource. Indeed, the unpredictable thrives in the filament and fiber of contemporary subjects such as pipe maker Mark Tinsky and bullfighter Raymond Ansotegui. Spreading from the past to the present,

Montana Eccentrics is the affirmation of a mantra: living in Montana isn't always easy, but sticking to the normal, ordinary path is way too hard.

SECTION ONE

A GALLERY OF BYGONE ECCENTRICS

James Presley Ball

1825-1904

Renowned Black Photographer in Helena

THE WIDELY CONVENTIONAL date for the birth of commercial photography is 1839, when Frenchman Louis-Jacques-Mandé Daguerre's invention of the daguerreotype was announced publicly. Within several years, black Americans were at the vanguard of this medium, including James Presley Ball who achieved great success in Cincinnati beginning in the 1850s, and who later lived and worked in Helena, Montana, between approximately 1887 and 1900.

Ball (1825-1904) dealt with rapidly evolving technologies, from the unwieldy daguerreotype in the 1840s to the simple, easy-to-duplicate photographic prints of the early 1900s.

Born free in Virginia, Ball said that he made his up mind to become a photographer in 1845 after "a chance meeting" with a black, Bostonian daguerreotypist named John B. Bailey.

In Cincinnati, Ball became proficient in a range of practices, including the ambrotype, the tintype, the stereotype, and the one named after Louis J.M. Daguerre, the popular daguerreotype.

In the early 1850s, Ball and his future brother-in-law, Alexander Thomas, formed "Ball & Thomas," which earned the reputation as "the finest photographic gallery west of the Allegheny Mountains," according to one contemporary newspaper. By 1853 Ball operated a well-equipped studio in downtown Cincinnati, which included the service of nine employees. "Ball's Great Daguerrian Gallery of the West," one of the most celebrated galleries in the United States, was

featured in a wood engrav-
ing in Gleason's Pictorial
Drawing-Room Compan-
ion, April 1, 1854. "The
most lifelike, the most beautiful, the most durable, the
cheapest"—that's what a
Ball advertisement prom-
ised the daguerreotype-
loving public.

In 1855, Bostonians had
something big to celebrate
in J.P. Ball's handiwork:
the 2,400-square-foot anti-
slavery photo panorama
"Ball's Splendid Mammoth
Pictorial Tour of the United
States, Comprising Views
of the African Slave Trade;
of Northern and Southern
Cities; of Cotton and Sugar
Plantations; of the Mississippi, Ohio, and Susque-

hanna Rivers, Niagara Falls, &C." The exhibit, on view at the
Boston Armory, was an outgrowth of Ball's antislavery work in
Cincinnati. Ball had a largely white clientele—many of them
active abolitionists and all of them undoubtedly sympathetic
to the anti-slavery movement. (Unfortunately, the exhibit did
not survive.)

In 1856, Ball passed through Europe, photographing,
among others, Queen Victoria and author Charles Dickens. As
Ball's status swelled, many renowned subjects appeared at his

Cincinnati studio, including distinguished abolitionist Frederick Douglass, Ulysses S. Grant's mother and sister, Swedish opera singer Jenny Lind, black orator Henry Highland Garnet, and several Union Army officers and soldiers.

Despite his reputation, Ball was perennially under the threat of asset liquidation and bankruptcy, so he moved to several towns and cities across the Midwest and rural south. In 1887, wanting to alleviate his persistent rheumatism in a drier climate, Ball arrived in Helena, Montana Territory, with his son, daughter, and daughter-in-law. Additionally, he sought to live in a western society that was more tolerant of blacks. (In 1882, voters in Helena passed a referendum ending segregated public schools. The next year, the territorial legislature repealed the segregation law for the entire territory.) The 1888 Helena City Directory lists the residence for father and son as 129 Broadway.

In 1870 there were about 180 persons "of full or partial black ancestry" in the Montana Territory, and by 1880 the number had approximately doubled to 356. But the highest proportion of blacks in Montana was in the territorial center of Helena, where in 1870 the black population was 2.3 percent of the city's total. Fort Benton and Butte contained the other highest concentrations of black people.

In December 1887, James Presley Ball was nominated as a delegate to a state civil rights convention and later ran for several offices on the Republican ticket. He later became president of Montana's Afro-American Club and co-founded the St. James AME Church (114 N Hoback Street, now a private residence). He was nominated for a county coroner position (which he declined).

His son, James Presley Ball Jr. was the editor of *The Colored Citizen*, the earliest of three newspapers published for black readers in Montana before World War I. (In 1900 black Americans represented only 1 percent (1,523) of the state population, but the community published two other newspapers, *The Montana Plaindealer* in Helena and *The New Age* in Butte.)

Ball, Jr. proclaimed in the inaugural issue, published on September 3, 1894, the paper's foundational philosophy and mission: "It cannot be denied that our people, through force of circumstance, occupy a peculiar status in this country. We are not thoroughly known. Our better qualities are not presented fairly to the public...Montana has a right to feel proud of its 2,500 colored citizens ...." Ball, Jr. added that the newspaper's reason for existence was "the intense interest among the city's 279 colored citizens" in the upcoming election to decide the site of the state capitol. (During the early 1890s, a battle was waged between the cities of Helena and Anaconda, over which would be chosen the capitol of the newly formed state.)

A full-page endorsement in the final issue of the newspaper on November 5, 1894, clarified the rationale for preferring Helena over Anaconda, in bold type: "The Anaconda Mining Company Does Not Employ a solitary colored man. Dagoes and Foreigners are preferred to Native Colored Americans. Vote for HELENA for Capitol." Helena came out victorious by less than 2,000 of the more than 52,000 votes cast.

The Colored Citizen was published at 137 N. Main St., the very location of Ball's portrait photography studio and residence for most of his career in Helena (currently the upper floor of what is the Goodkind Building at Sixth and Main, sometimes called the Broadwater Block).

The Colored Citizen, September 3, 1894, praised the elder's reputation:

"Helena enjoys the notoriety of having the only colored photographer in the Northwest. Mr. J. P. Ball who has had a

studio here for a number of years, has a large patronage among
many of our best citizens. He is one of the oldest members now
in the profession, dating back to 1845, the famous daguerreotype era, and has had the satisfaction of taking numerous
medals for superior work over many of the most skillful and
artistic competitions in the largest eastern cities. Prior to,
during, and for several years after, the war Mr. Ball had one of
the largest and best equipped studios in Cincinnati."

Ball photographed business leaders, immigrants, pioneers,
and—most disturbingly—the lynching of a black man named
William Biggerstaff. Not much is known about Biggerstaff
except that he was "born a slave in 1854, in Lexington, Ky." He
was convicted of killing "Dick" Johnson after an argument that
took place on June 9, 1895. Biggerstaff pleaded self-defense.
The hanging took place on April 6, 1896; the "weight fell at
10:08 a.m. in Helena courtyard." In a succession of photographs, Biggerstaff is first pictured in a suit, flower pinned to
lapel, handkerchief in pocket. The next sequence is Biggerstaff
being hanged, the dangling, hooded man attended to by the
Reverend Victor Day and by Sheriff Henry Jurgens. Finally,
he is displayed in a coffin.

Only J.P. Ball & Son seem to have photographed the laying
of the cornerstone of the State Capitol building by grand
master Charles W. Pomeroy. Although a simple collection,
the photographs reveal Ball's vigorous esthetic sensibilities in
the plethora of umbrellas. In his photos, the umbrellas make
rhythmic, arching patterns—apparently more interesting to the
Balls than the audience itself—that bring to mind the similar
use of this motif in 19th-century Japanese prints.

Some of Ball's most mysterious photos are his undated
images of the Ming merchant family, once among Helena's
wealthiest pioneers and land investors. Other than a date of

1891 to 1900, however, the specific details of these photos are lost to history. In other images, Bell employed the inventive use of photographic montage: framing the heads in a scallop shell.

In late-1900, James Presley Ball followed his son, J.P. Ball Jr., to Seattle and eventually settled in Honolulu, opening a studio in his home, which was co-operated by his daughter, Estella. His obituary stated that Ball died in 1904 of rheumatism.

Reverend William "Brother Van" Orsdel

1848-1919

The Grand Old Man of Methodism

REVEREND WILLIAM ORSDEL was an apostle and an evangelist, as well as a performer and an entertainer. Oftentimes, he fulfilled all four roles in the very same saloon or dance hall. From Bannack to Billings and Virginia City to Havre, the circuit-riding preacher left a colorful mark on Montana's history, credited with covering more than 50,000 square miles and building more than 100 Methodist churches and parsonages in Montana under his tenure.

A typical story about the life and times of the man affectionately known as "Brother Van" could be gleaned in the news archives of his trip to Bannack in the 1870s, while it was at the crest of gold and silver mining activity. Covering the state by saddle horse, he found all the gambling houses and bars bristling with patrons one Sunday evening. Stepping up to the saloon, he announced himself as a Man of God and, since the town had no church assembly, he asked the saloon owner if he could hold service on the premises, right away.

The bartender whistled the packs of beer guzzlers and hell raisers to shush the noise. He announced that the business would be closed for the next hour and that the mysteriously charming preacher would be conducting sermon instead.

On this particular night, Brother Van had the gathering's rapt attention, and he chose to sing a popular song of the period, "Diamonds in the Rough," his "rich, booming voice" permeating the house. The crowd, "hungry for entertainment," was reported to have "loved the song and asked for more." Years later, the miners who were inspired by Brother Vance built the Grace Methodist Church at Bannack. Dedicated in August of 1877, the church is one of the approximately 50 buildings that now comprise Bannack State Park.

Origins of "Brother Van"

THE SON OF FARMERS, William Wesley Van Orsdel was born near Gettysburg, Pennsylvania, on March 20, 1848. At age 15 he observed the horrors of the gruesome three-day battle of Gettysburg, with more than 50,000 total casualties. (Two of his brothers were Civil War veterans.) On several occasions he later sermonized on the memories of being present in the crowd while he listened to Abraham Lincoln's "Gettysburg Address" on November 19, 1863. His origins as a Christian worker were harsh: orphaned at age 12, he embraced the Methodist church of his parents and its doctrines and teachings. While employed as an engineer of a stationary engine in the oil fields of Pennsylvania, Orsdel took up revivals and found purpose as a revivalist.

In 1872 he came to Montana by way of the Missouri River, arriving on a riverboat called the *Far West* that deposited him in Idaho. It seems that the 24-year-old adventurer's first day and service in Montana was spent some time in June 1872 preaching to trappers, rivermen and merchants and their families in Fort Benton, perhaps at a saloon near the dock of the Missouri. That summer or fall he held services in Fort Shaw and Sun River, the latter event immortalized by Charles M. Russell in one of the cowboy artist's earliest paintings.

Fulfilling his vision of "God's power and man's need," as he once said, "Brother Van" would spend the remainder of his life serving the people of Montana. His first "official assignment" came in the summer of 1873 when he was appointed as junior preacher on "the Virginia City-Bannack circuit" with Rev. Francis Riggin. His circuit encompassed typical frontier towns, including the capital of the Montana Territory, Virginia City, and the developing region in the vicinity of Sheridan, Twin Bridges, and Dillon. Brother Van traveled on horseback, preaching during weeknights and holding services at various schoolhouses and private homes in southern Montana and Idaho. He also held revivals.

According to one account, Brother Van and Rev. Riggin served about 18 Methodist Church congregants "in an area covering 200 miles from east to west and 50 miles from north to south." Rev. Riggin would deliver the sermon, and Brother Van would give "the emotional alter call."

There are many spectacular stories of Brother Van, and perhaps a few of them to some extent have been embroidered through the years. One much repeated tale has Brother Van arriving in the Montana Territory without a horse, "walking 75 miles from Bozeman to Radersburg." When he arrived "tired and covered in dust," people thought they captured the horse thief from a wanted poster, who had a $100 dollar reward on his back. Brother Van realized he was in trouble when guns were drawn and a hanging noose was unfurled, so he started singing "O Happy Day," said a prayer, and then introduced himself as Brother Van, a singer and a man of prayer, not a thief. His bit of quick-thinking theatrics worked, for "the town welcomed the new preacher."

Another larger-than-life tale claims that Brother Van was on a stagecoach that was blocked by a band of road agents. As the passengers were lined up and the robbers looted their cash and valuables, the thief frisked Brother Van, who, at that point, reportedly asked, "You wouldn't rob me, would you? I'm just a poor Methodist preacher!" The robber, it was said, replied, "Of course not. I'm a Methodist myself."

Several accounts reference Brother Van's relationship with the Native Americans as friendly, especially with the Blackfeet Indians, who reportedly invited him to accompany them on a buffalo hunt. In several depictions Brother Van is portrayed as a willing Indian Scout. In August of 1877, Chief Joseph and the Nez Perce tribesmen had fought four major battles with General Gibbon and his troops at the Battle of the Big Hole and were headed south. Frightened that the Indians would attack them next, the people of Bannack gathered one and all into town. Word soon arrived of an attack on a nearby ranch. A large group of men, including Brother Van, were then sent to save the residents—though it was too late. The bodies of several men murdered in the attack were brought to Bannack where services were held.

According to one account, Brother Van and another man named John Poindexter then volunteered to ride out and inform General Howard of the threatening advancement of the tribes. "Howard dispatched a full company of Calvary to Bannack and sent a message with the two men to be given to a stage driver who would then give it to a telegrapher who would send the message to military headquarters in Washington D.C."

After a long, uncertain trek, Brother Van and Poindexter finally returned to Bannack to find Captain Ball with a
company of cavalry guarding Bannack. With him was W.A.
Clark in command of two companies of Butte volunteers. No
more large-scale attacks ever happened at Bannack, and Brother
Van's gallantry earned him the respect of its residents.

Legacy of "Brother Van"

SENATOR THOMAS CHARLES POWERS of Helena once met
Brother Van at a church service in Fort Benton, and he later
shared his impressions of hearing him preach a sermon in a
log cabin with a dirt roof. According to one quote attributed
to Powers, Brother Van was an open-minded man who was
singularly preoccupied with his career. "His audience was
made up of freighters, traders, prospectors, miners and Indians. Brother Van loved them all. There was no caste in this
man's religion. He loved all people, no matter what their color
or language might be."

In 1888 Brother Van helped establish Montana Wesleyan
University in Helena (no longer operating as a college). On July
4, 1902, he gave the prayer at the dedication for the newly built
state capital in Helena. Brother Van also oversaw the establish-
ment of several hospitals. In 1909 the Montana Preparatory
Deaconess School for Children opened, which continues today
as the Intermountain Children's Services for emotionally challenged children.

The parsonage of the First United Methodist Church of
Great Falls was considered to be home by Brother Van, or the
closest thing to it for such an itinerant. It was built in 1909, and
the pastor made sure it included accommodations for Brother
Van, a place where he could keep his few belongings, have a

break, and be included as part of the pastor's family. Busily crossing the plains, summits, and frontiers of the immense state, he stayed there only a couple nights a month. Now it is listed on the National Registry of Historic Places and includes a museum dedicated to Brother Van and Methodist church history in Montana. Among the approximately 100 churches and 50 parsonages credited to his work is the Van Orsdel Methodist Church in Havre.

The Rev. William Wesley Van Orsdel passed away December 19, 1919, in the Montana Deaconess Hospital in Great Falls and shortly thereafter was interred in Forestvale Cemetery in Helena. At a eulogy for Brother Van, one reverend, who had spent many years side by side and saddle by saddle with the passionate preacher, had this to say about him:

"He was a bachelor and a wanderer, and he spent his life among us preaching the gospel of hope and good cheer, a gospel of love; building churches and schools, hospitals, parsonages and deaconess homes, until it did not matter where he went, he was welcome. He started big work among us as a youngman, and finished it as a white haired and reverend father of the whole church, and a power in the religious life of the commonwealth. He rolled up a record of devotion to humanity, to the uplift of society, to the foundation of religions and charitable organizations, and to the cause of religion seldom matched in the west."

LEWIS DUNCAN

(1857-1936)

The Mayor Who Flew The
Red Flag Over Butte

LEWIS J. DUNCAN WAS A LAWYER, book agent, minister, lecturer, and, most notably, a politician of a radical faith whose party experienced its briefest glory years in Montana in the early 1900s.

The man who flew the red flag in Butte was born in St. Louis, Missouri, on May 4, 1857. His father, Edwin Duncan, was a New Yorker of Scotch ancestry. His mother, Emma Francis Duncan, was born in England and raised in Illinois starting from the age of 10. After the death of his father, the family moved to Illinois and located at Quincy, where he received his public education. After attending Hanover College in Indiana, he entered the railway service as an accountant and later became a certified public accountant. He read vigorously and sold books. Then he took up the study of law, married the daughter of a well-known lawyer, and was admitted to the Illinois bar in 1878.

After two years, he gave up his law practice to become a Unitarian minister at Sheffield, Illinois. He founded the Church of Good Will in nearby Streator and moved to a pastor's position at the Milwaukee Ethical Society.

Lewis was called to Butte to become pastor of the Unitarian church in 1902. His arrival was delayed two years by the illness of a daughter, who passed away in Milwaukee. He continued to follow the clerical profession in the mining town until March

1910, when he lost his job amid terrible labor and political strife. The Socialist publication, the *International Socialist Review*, described the circumstances of his job loss (through leftist lenses):

"Really, he lost his job as a preacher because he would not obey orders. He was the one public man in Butte that had the courage to take the platform in favor of (Charles A.) Moyer, (Bill) Haywood, and (George) Pettibone, when they were on trial (1907) in Idaho for their lives. That act alone almost cost him his meal ticket, but Lewis J. Duncan is not a quitter. Sometime later, when Emma Goldman was billed to speak in Butte, and the use of the halls in the city was denied her, Preacher Duncan offered her the use of his church and lost his job."

According to Duncan's own version of the resignation, he defined his eight years as a preacher in Butte as an epoch "of hardship and struggle." People with "capitalistic minds," he said, would not support his preaching. "Since the Unitarian Hierarchy was also apathetic about my work with the people, I had to get out," he later said.

One Montana newspaper described Duncan's departure rather diplomatically. "His sermons were powerful and popular, and he soon was in demand as a public speaker. Some of his utterances at labor gatherings caused discussion in his congregation and he resigned, in 1910."

The next year found him the person in charge of the

Montana Socialist Party, of which he served as the office of secretary for $75 per month. He received the endorsement of the Butte local wing of the party and ran for the mayor of Butte. Opposition to his election was trivial since he wasn't predicted to be much of a factor in it. However, Duncan benefited from a fundamental lack of trust among the working-class people of Butte towards both major parties, Democratic and Republican, who were increasingly viewed as two heads of the same corrupt, ineffective, condescendingly elite.

Duncan was elected in April 1911, tallying 4,269 votes, edging the leading Democrat (2,435 votes) and Republican (1,293), and becoming one of the first socialists to achieve that office in an American city of importance. (What transpired in Butte was not an isolated episode for socialists in America at the time. According to one contemporary publication, in 1910 socialists "were voted to office in 57 communities in 24 states," including Victor Berger of Wisconsin to the U.S. House of Representatives.)

Duncan's victory, a self-touted workers' government, marked the apex of the Socialist movement in Butte and perhaps even Montana, gains he detailed in the April 1912 party handbook: "We have carried on a constructive and impartial administration, given a clean, honest and efficient city government, conducted the city economically, restored its financial credit, and made it a healthier and more wholesome habitation."

His re-election campaign cited a lower budget than Butte had seen in years and a sharp reduction in deaths from all causes, including contagious diseases. He was re-elected handily in 1913, a plurality of more than 600 votes. Lewis was the first Butte mayor to succeed himself.

He was a member of the national committee of the socialist party, "one of the profound thinkers of his political faith," is how one party pamphlet referenced him, and served as a delegate to the socialist national convention in Indianapolis, in 1912. He lectured frequently upon socialism and the corruption and inefficiency of standard municipal governments, and he typed several pamphlets and contributed magazine articles on socialist doctrine.

According to one contemporary account, "Mayor Duncan attracted wide attention for his opposition to certain accepted socialist party methods. He led an unsuccessful minority in that convention, but that contention forced the party to take an advanced position in respect to tactics and relations with economic organizations."

Lewis was the editor of the Butte Socialist, and of the Montana Socialist, and was first secretary-treasurer of the Butte Socialist Publishing company. He belonged to the Workingmen's union of Butte, the A.F. and A.M. labor organizations, and he represented his union for several terms in the Silver Bow Trades and Labor council.

On July 3, 1914, Duncan was attacked in his City Hall office by a deranged Finnish miner named Erik Lantala, described "as an avowed Socialist," who harbored an imagined political grudge against the mayor. Duncan was slashed three times with a large knife before he shot his assailant to death.

He served until October 6, 1914, when he and Sheriff Tim Driscoll were removed from office through dismissal proceedings growing out of summer rioting that had resulted in the dissolution of Butte Miners Union No. 11 W.F.M. Both men were found guilty of the charges brought against them, an "alleged refusal or neglect to perform (their) duties...in connection with the disorders on and after June 13, 1914." Duncan claimed the proceedings a political coup, retaliation for his refusal to not subordinate human life to property interests. Sans a third run for mayor in 1917 that resulted in a devastating defeat, he would never return to the political arena.

Following his removal from office he worked in the mines and at the copper boilers in Butte, but he was too frail bodily to perform this required labor and accepted a congregational call to South Dakota. Eventually, he removed to Minnesota, where he was engaged in newspaper work for two years, after which he dedicated himself to private teaching. His subjects ranged from English and business to the fields of science, to public speaking, dramatics, and music. Finally poor constitution compelled him to retire from active work.

He died on January 24, 1936, of pneumonia, in hospital at Rochester, Minnesota.

BARTENDER JULIAN ANDERSON

(1860-1962)

The Master of Mixes

HE WAS QUICK WITH A QUIP or to lend a sympathetic ear. He was fast to light a cigar or laugh at a wisecrack. But most significantly, he could whip up an unforgettable absinthe cocktail or old fashion gin or whiskey cocktail with unnatural ease.

He was the "Master of Mixes," a much-admired bartender at the Montana Club who served thousands of drinks to hundreds of local members as well as a smattering of true notables throughout his 60-year tenure.

Julian Anderson asserted that he was born in Hamburg, Germany, where his parents moved "with wealthy Virginia plantation owners who were fleeing the Civil War," although there is no record of his birth in that country. Similarly, when it comes to determining his age, printed or attributed dates seem to be at loggerheads. Nonetheless, his most probably birth date was September 23, 1860.

"I observe September 23rd as my birthday, because my mother told me I was born at 'fodder-pulling time,'" Anderson said once.

At the age of six or seven, his family returned to the United States and Virginia, quite possibility the first time that Julian heard his native tongue beyond the conversations of his parents. The Andersons later decamped to Washington DC before they pressed on to Denver, Colorado. His time out west seems to have been a formative period in young Julian's life,

for it is where he claimed to have first tasted his independence, and it's also where he got his first job as a bell hop at the American House (in Denver) and learned how to work as a baker and confectioner (in Laramie, Wyoming).

He came to Helena in either the winter of 1886 or spring of 1887. (Some accounts claim he arrived in Helena while "still in his teens in 1887," but this would invalidate his birthdate as taking place at the time of the Civil War.)

Presumably, it was a much older Anderson who would've come to Helena, working first for James Sullivan, "who was later mayor" and who "ran the town's best barbershop," Julian once said. He then worked for Thomas O'Brien and Son, proprietors of the Merchant's Hotel, (later the Monticello, no longer extant) as a porter. When the hotel went bankrupt, W.A. Brown, the receiver, took over, making Anderson manager.

The following summer he became night clerk at the Broadwater Hotel.

While Julian was a bit forgetful as to identifying the precise dates and periods of his life, he later recalled his one season at the Broadwater coinciding with "the time they had the fight about where the capital was going to be." (Referendums were held in 1892 and 1894 to settle on the state's capital; the result was to keep the capitol in Helena.)

In June 1893, he went to the newly minted Montana Club as bartender for what he recalls as being "a very exclusive club of men."

Behind the polished mahogany of the Montana Club bar was where he stood for virtually the remainder of his life, staying on until 1953, when he retired as one of the Queen City of the Rockies' most recognizable characters.

At that time, the Montana Club soared above the cityscape; though before long blocks of five-story buildings pushed up in the fledgling capital (statehood was granted a few years earlier in 1889). Initial members included selected (all-male) individuals in mining, farming, timber, law, banking, transportation and wholesale goods. According to club reports, "Fifty constituents became nearly 300 members within six years."

An arson fire decimated the Montana Club in April 1913. The blaze, set by Anderson's 14-year-old son, Harry, started on the sixth floor but extended swiftly.

Insurance didn't even cover the full $150,000 damage; however, club members quickly gathered enough money to build a new clubhouse shortly after the fire. Minnesota-born architect Cass Gilbert, who became known as "father of the skyscraper" and also designed the Minnesota, Arkansas and West Virginia Capitals, went to work on the restructured design. Despite the fact that his own son caused the incident, Anderson smilingly persevered, continuing to shake well, strain, drop the cherries in, and serve.

In 1918, Helena was purportedly home to "at least 65 saloons," according to one newspaper account. One of the city's fanciest drinking establishments, the Rathskeller, or basement beer hall, offered an elevated level of coziness, which included expensive reproduction leather, lavish coats of arms symbols and floor-to-ceiling paneling fashioned from Washington fir.

Prohibition in Montana went into effect at the end of 1918, which was two years before national prohibition, and during this period Montana Club members kept their own cabinets of clandestine liquor down in the cellar bar; Anderson held the key to their stashes and would fix drinks for patrons using their personal reserves. (The Twenty-first Amendment to the U.S. Constitution, ratified on December 5, 1933, repealed the Eighteenth Amendment and ended national Prohibition.)

During his tenure, Anderson garnered local fame as the master of mixes. Known for his warm, informal friendliness, disarming smile, and his connoisseur's precision, Julian twisted each sprig of mint and polished every glass with inestimable pride. Even though he was an adept drink technician—concocting everything from champagne punch bowls for a party of fifty, to unique Montana Club martini cocktails—he often said that he "never" took a drink himself.

"The proudest moment in my life was the time I served Teddy Roosevelt," Anderson told a local newspaper in 1950. "He was President then (serving between 1901 and 1909) and about the biggest man in the world. Everyone respected him and his word was generally law, but he was kind and pleasant to me." He even said that he heard Teddy say "dee-lighted" in person.

President Roosevelt was but one of the many prominent figures served by Anderson at the Club. Humorist Mark Twain, actor Otis Skinner, artist Charlie Russell, and politician William Jennings Bryan were also served with one of Anderson's recipes. Other notables were foreign princes and domestic copper kings, including Prince Albert of Belgium, Prince Olaf of Norway, W.A. Clark, F. Augustus Heinze, and Marcus Daly.

Anderson's residence on 613 E. Broadway served as a constant hub for the city's small African American community for decades. First platted in 1887, Anderson purchased the property in 1913, though census records reveal that he had lived there even earlier.

City directories list the Anderson family at 613 E. Broadway by 1910, and that year census takers cataloged the household. At the time it included Julian, age listed as 44 (which would again mean Julian was born after the Civil War and not in 1859 or 1860 as he later claimed), and working as a "steward" at the Montana Club, and his 41-year-old wife Margaret, whom he'd married in Helena in 1888. It also included their seven children, all of whom were born in Montana, ranging in ages from 21 to one-year-old.

Sometime thereafter Julian and Margaret divorced, and in 1915 Julian remarried Tennessee -born Ella Newton Davis, 25. By 1930, inhabitants included son Julian Anderson Jr. and his Missouri -born wife Mattie, 45, who worked as a "chamber maid" at a "club house," as well as daughter Elenorah and her husband of three years, Ad Edison Banks, a native Alabaman who worked as "a porter at a hotel."

Throughout all this change, Anderson continued to shake and stir, even authoring a recipe guide of his most popular mixes. In 1938, members celebrated Julian's forty-fifth anniversary with the club, signing a tribute to him that announced: "To Julian Anderson who never forgets us, is always constant, pleasant and competent."

By 1940, Anderson was a widower, and he was taking in African American lodgers who made their living working in the local service industry.

On June 20, 1953, Anderson was honored for 60 years of service at the Montana Club at a board of governors' dinner and later feted at a reception by hundreds of club members. Around that time, the bartender who had become one of Helena's most familiar institutions, retired from service.

Years later, newspapers reported that he celebrated his 99th birthday at a family dinner party at home and enjoyed his favorite cake—pound cake, without icing—with nine red and green candles on each side. Julian said that at one time he chewed tobacco but never smoked or imbibed in alcoholic beverages. He attributed his longevity to clean living and plenty of nimbleness. Yearly, he cultivated a vegetable garden at his backyard, scratching earth and sprinkling seeds.

Julian Anderson died on December 20, 1962 at the purported though unverifiable age of close to 102.

D.J. O'MALLEY

(1867-1943)

Cowboy Poet of Miles City

Sometimes wholly spontaneous, sometimes sung with original lines fused to existing tunes, D.J. O'Malley's songs of light-hearted leisure were something his rough-hewn cowpoke cohorts came to admire, and his rhymes provided a much-appreciated entertainment after the hard day's drudgery on the range was complete.

D.J. O'Malley was a legend. Indeed, he was the last survivor of the more than 400 cowboys who attended the first-ever roundup at Miles City, in 1881. In the early 1880s, O'Malley, a boy of 14, had already become "a full-fledged cowboy," as he described himself. Much later, in 1939, he was the guest of honor at the first annual Reunion of the Range Riders Association, made up of the range riders who rode the trails in those early days, from 1881 to 1890.

O'Malley's Montana

The son of a Civil War soldier who died years after sustaining a combat wound, O'Malley was born in New York City in 1867.

He spent his early boyhood in Texas but came to Montana in 1877, the place he would call home for more than forty years. Despite later wanderings across the Midwest, where he died in 1943, he specified that his burial site had to be in eastern Montana.

Many of his earli-
est memories, O'Malley
recalled, were of "two frontier outposts, Fort Dodge
and Fort Larned, both in
Kansas," and later outposts
in Wyoming and Montana.
According to O'Malley's
journals, his stepfather,
Charles White served in the
19th Infantry in the U.S.
Army, completing his enlist-
ment in the infantry at Fort
Larned in 1875. White then went to Fort Sanders in Wyoming
where he joined Troop E of the Second Cavalry. In October,
1877 the regiment and the White family moved to Fort Keogh,
near Miles City, 130 miles north of the site of the fateful Battle
of the Little Big Horn; Custer's last stand had taken place in
the summer of the previous year.

Sometime in the mid-1880s, Charles A. White's family—
his stepfather's own path is murky—D.J., his mother, and his
siblings relocated to Miles City.

As a boy of 11, O'Malley recalled his first meeting with
General Nelson A. Miles, then a colonel, at Fort Keogh.
O'Malley went to school with the General's two children, Sher-
man and Cecelia, at the fort.

He also met soldier and later showman William "Buffalo
Bill" Cody, and was acquainted with other famous scouts and
adventurers of that pioneer era, including Luther "Yellowstone" Kelley. O'Malley was also friendly with a number of
young army lieutenants at Fort Keogh, many of whom went
on to illustrious careers, including West Point graduate Hunter

Liggett, who later would serve as second in command to General Pershing in Europe during the World War.

While at Fort Keogh O'Malley also made the acquaintance of many of the stalwart Indian chiefs who took part in the Battle of the Little Bighorn in 1876, when the entire Custer command was annihilated by the Lakota and other Plains Indians. Among these chiefs were Rain-in-the-Face, American Horse, Spotted Elk, (Sioux) Two Moon, Little Wolf, Fire Crow, High Walking (Cheyenne) Chief Gall, Many Horses (Sioux)) and many others.

Working as "A Rep"

O'MALLEY LATER RECALLED that for several years Fort Keogh— strategically constructed at the interchange of the Yellowstone and Tongue Rivers—was the site of "intermittent Indian warfare," which ostensibly made it "an exciting place for a boy just entering his teens."

Violence and upheaval, stemming from the removal and resettlement of Indian tribes, were core elements of the day. O'Malley lived at the fort until 1881; many of things that he observed and internalized later shaped his poetry and journalism.

O'Malley rode the subsequent 19 years as a cowboy, joining the N Bar N outfit as a horse wrangler at age 14 and working for many years as a cowpuncher at large known as "a rep." A rep worked outside the home front steering the direction of cattle and otherwise "looking after the interests of the outfit he represented."

Here's how O'Malley described the job in his journals: "A "rep" had to have good character, reliability, good judgment and tact, because his word was law with respect to calves branded, beef shipped and many other details of the business.

He had to be a good mixer, and he had to know brands."

He was christened the nickname N Bar N Kid and "Kid White" (his stepfather's name was White); and later the "Cowboy Poet," because of his fondness for writing poetry and song with a wild, western relish.

The "Cowboy Poet"

SEVERAL COUNTRY-COWBOY music encyclopedias credit O'Malley with a few different compositions that have seemingly endured the standard of time. At least four of O'Malley's poems are said to be well circulated "wherever there is interest in western range songs," says one source. These are listed as "Sweet By and By Revised," "A Cowboy's Death," "After the Roundup," and the "D 2 Horse Wrangler."

According to a mid-century edition of True West, "Sweet By and By Revised" represented one of O'Malley's initial attempts at writing lines. Said the author:

"He (O'Malley) said that it was probably the third or fourth poem of the forty or more that he wrote while cowpunching. These rough set of verses apparently furnished the foundation for the ballad often called "The Cowboy's Dream," which has been given a place in nearly every collection of American frontier songs." O'Malley told True West that he received the inspiration for his verses from one of the N Bar N cowhands.

The magazine reprinted the original five verses as jotted down by O'Malley in the early 1880's.

Tonight as I lay on the prairie
Looking up at the stars in the sky,
I wonder if ever a cowboy
Will get to that sweet by and by.

For the trail to that bright mystic region
Is both narrow and dim, so they say,
While the broad one that leads to perdition
Is posted and blazed all the way.
Now I wonder whose fault that so many
Will be lost at the great final day,
When they might have been rich and had plenty
Had they known of the dim narrow way.

In addition to his penchant for poetry, O'Malley wrote extensively on western subjects and on incidents in which he was involved or experienced.

Last Trail

THE LAST TRAIL DRIVE he took part in was in 1891, from Texas to Montana. O'Malley recalled three trips taken by himself over the trail with southern cattle from Texas bound for the northern ranges in Montana. After the N Bar N sold out in 1896, he worked for various Montana outfits, among them the Bow and Arrow, M Diamond, Half Circle L and L U Bar. He also worked as deputy stock inspector for the Stock Growers' Association under one Billy Smith. In 1904 he served as special deputy sheriff at Rosebud, under John Gibb, sheriff of Custer County. Later he was a guard at the State Penitentiary at Deer Lodge. In 1909, at age 43, he went east to Eau Claire, Wisconsin, married and in later years made his home there.

He didn't forget Montana, however, and the sentiment was reciprocated. In 1939, he was the guest of honor at the first annual reunion of the Range Riders association. In 1941 and 1942 he again was again the guest of honor at the reunions.

At age 70 O'Malley was employed at the tire plant of Gillette

Rubber Company, but he was forced to give this up when "his heart began troubling him," according to his obituary in one Wisconsin newspaper. The final few years of his life were spent raising raspberries on a plot of ground on Crescent Avenue, in Eau Claire.

When he passed in 1943 D.J. O'Malley's body was taken to Miles City for burial. Not only was he directly linked to so many of the historic characters of what is often categorized as the Old West, O'Malley left his own distinctive footprint upon Montana's pioneer era.

Jack Munroe

(1877-1942)

Pugilist-Prospector-Writer-Soldier

AT THE BEGINNING of the twentieth century, Jack Munroe made a distinct mark on the smoky city of Butte, Montana.

Like other men of similar destiny, he scraped out a living in the deep choking cramp of the copper mines. But in addition to his ability to withstand the toil of stoop labor, this brawny itinerant possessed an unusual amount of courage.

When the world heavyweight boxing champion was passing through, Munroe had the gumption and random luck to challenge him to an exhibition—a confrontation that thrilled his hometown and cemented his status among the local populace as a hero.

Born in 1877 in Nova Scotia, Canada, he followed his older brother and an uncle south to the United States, "one of a dozen Cape Breton Island natives who decamped in the west to mine copper in Montana," according to one account.

At age 18 he was said to be a member of the Butte city adult football team. He was later a guard on San Francisco's Olympic Club football team. In 1900, he won the Olympic club amateur heavyweight championship medal by defeating three men. Sometime thereafter, Munroe started boxing professionally, all while continuing to play football and working odd, errant jobs.

Heavyweight Gauntlet Thrown Down

THE PERIPATETIC MINER-boxer returned to the Butte area sometime around 1903. Sweating out a precarious living six days a week, ten hours a day, in what most considered unrestrained misery on earth, didn't seem to impede the will of Munroe. One night in December, 1903, he was purportedly "one of a bunch of the vagabond miners who were carousing in the bars and streets of Butte, itching for a little excitement," according to one boxing historian's account. The heavyweight boxing champion Jim Jeffries, born in Ohio in 1875, and the older ex-champion Bob Fitzsimmons, born in England in 1863, were in Butte, too.

According to an article about Munroe in *Macleans*, "In Munroe's time (and about the time he challenged Jeffries), professional prizefighting was still illegal almost everywhere in North America and, over the whole "sport," there still hung the bloody, sweaty aroma of the bad. old, bareknuckle days of eye-gouging, armbreaking. neck-chopping, ear-biting, groin-smashing and snappy tricks to dislocate elbows, cave in ribs and crunch faces."

The gauntlet was thrown down (by whom and in what context is a matter of conjecture): any man who could with-stand four rounds with Jeffries or Fitzsimmons would receive

$500. The amount of the bet varies in alternate accounts, but this figure seems to be most oft repeated.

According to the *Butte Miner*, no event of the year had attracted so much attention as Jeffries' Butte experience with Munroe in December of 1903. "All the big newspapers east and west have been keeping the wires busy asking for extended accounts of the four-round bout, pictures and measurements of Munroe and his history. In addition to the *Associated Press* reports many papers asked for specials."

The sparring exhibition at the Broadway theater took place on the Saturday night subsequent to the challenge, drawing "a fifteen-hundred-dollar house," according to the *Butte Miner*. The fighters were operating under Marquis of Queensberry rules, with clean breaking and no hitting in the clinches.

Jack Munroe: "Lion of the Hour in Butte"

AS IT TURNED OUT, on December 19, 1903, both fighters fulfilled their stated missions.

There are two schools of thought concerning the four-round affair between the champion and miner-pugilist. One is that Jeffries tried his best, but simply couldn't dispatch the clever, hardy opponent; the other is that it was a pre-arranged affair and that it was "fixed" for Munroe to withstand the limit. It's also possible that neither of these general beliefs would be correct; Jeffries might have considered the fight more of a lark than a serious threat, at least at first.

According to one ringside newspaperman, "Both men went into the ring in good faith, Munroe to do his best to stay the limit and Jeff to give the crowd some excitement."

At six feet and 195 pounds, the powerful miner fended off the champion—who was taller and outweighed him by at least

20 pounds—four rounds. Jeffries seemed to have done his meanest to stop Munroe. But he failed.

According to one ringside report, "Jeffries several times ignored the (Marquis of Queensbury) rule, and freely punched Munroe while in the clinches, and went at him rough shod, with the intention of stopping the affair as soon as possible. Several times he forced Munroe to his knees, but the Butte man took advantage of the count and rested up."

Of course, Munroe, with only a few professional bouts to his credit (though he had gone the limit with heavyweight champion Jack Johnson), was no equal for the champion, and his victory was not expected. (One account indentifies Munroe as "two years removed having laced boxing gloves and stepping into a ring to compete.")

But Munroe, who according to one account, trained exclusively for 10 straight days prior to the fight and was of "perfect wind, hard muscles, healthy pink flesh," showed gumption and pluck. Not content to survive, he even exhibited some aggressiveness, "landing several hard stiff jabs on the champion's nose."

Jeffries was "not altogether pleased" with the decision given by Referee Dune McDonald. This decision was recorded in his fight record as a losing mark, the first blight in his pugilistic career. Jeffries later blamed his defeat on a number of reasons, admitting that he underestimated his opponent, claiming he was out of condition, and even stating that he was afraid of exerting himself too strenuously in the unaccustomed elevation.

Similarly, the *Butte InterMountain* accused Jeffries of loafing, of being "hog-fat and easily winded in the high altitude" while Munroe "trained faithfully" for his fight with the champion.

Nonetheless, going the distance with Jeffries turned Munroe into a popular entity in the streets and taverns of Butte. "At present Munroe is the lion of the hour in Butte and through his unflinching grit has made many friends," stated the *Butte InterMountain* on December 22, 1903.

According to Macleans, "Eleven days later the Terrible Miner appeared in a vaudeville melodrama called Road To Ruin."

Munroe continued to box and two years later, on August 26, 1904, he accepted the rematch with the revengeful Jeffries. Despite the support Munroe received from a notable team of trainers, "Jeffries wiped the floor with the suddenly terrible miner," almost "decapitating" him with the first punch of the fight. Since the fight transpired in California, Munroe no longer had the hometown support of rowdy Butte folks and the crowd of 21,000 maintained no allegiance to him. He was reduced to a bruised, bloody heap of humanity within minutes, and the fight was called off to save his hide.

Munroe fought six more bouts after his title tilt with Jeffries—including a knockout loss to Jack Johnson in 1905— before retiring with a career mark of 9-2-4, with eight of those wins coming from KOs.

Prospector and Soldier of Fortune

MUNROE WASN'T QUITE FINISHED, however. He later beat Peter Maner, the Irish heavyweight champion, after he had returned to his native Nova Scotia. Subsequently, he found work as a prospector and lumberjack in Northern Ontario and signed up in Prince Patricia's Canadian Light Infantry at the onset of World War I. During training, he carried his double-bitted axe (it's reported that he later killed at least one German soldier with it) at his side. The regiment's mascot was a large collie named Bobby Burns; Munroe brought along the dog, it's been said, to provide color and a few smiles to counterweight the grimness of battle. Still, the war's harsh realities were undeniable, and an infected wound from a sniper's bullet led to the amputation of Munroe's right arm.

Following The Great War, Jack Munroe purportedly made gobs of wealth while returning to prospecting in his native Canada. He served as mayor of Elk Lake, Ontario, and even wrote a novel about his war experiences—recalling Bobby Burns, the bullet wound, the subsequent Military Cross honors—before dying at the age of 64 in February of 1942.

Blackfeet Sculptor John Louis Clarke

(1881-1970)

Speaking In Carvings

John Louis Clarke, an esteemed Blackfeet sculptor, found refuge in art as he overcame his deafness and muteness to produce a formidable body of work from his East Glacier studio

A carver of craggy animals, his stony, weather-beaten face practically seemed engraved, too. His lined hands, flowing with fluency, were hearty and coarse like oak or boulder, and no less substantial.

He had been robbed of the ability to speak or hear, yet his was a life without margins. By way of nimble fingers and fixed eyes, he felt the urge of the senses, scrounging ordinary wood that he hewed and chipped deeply, lovingly, with the characteristics of his own spirit and that of his subject matters.

Indeed, John Louis Clarke's physical deficiencies did not handicap his eloquence in sculpting or painting. Perhaps, conversely, something about that silence bestowed him with an indomitable outlet for his interior emotions, a conduit which speech might not have ever been able to adequately or wholly express.

Learning the Language of Art

The son of Horace and Margaret Clarke, John Clarke was born into history near Highwood, about 25 miles east of Great

Falls, in 1881. Sources vary as to his exact birthdate, but Clarke himself listed March 23, 1881 in a letter written in 1964.

His father, Horace John Clarke, was half Blackfeet, the son of Malcolm Clarke, a classmate and friend of Civil War General William Tecumseh Sherman.

According to a biographer of the Clarke family, Malcolm Clarke was a famous pioneer fur trader who "bought a toll road between Prickly Pear Canyon and Helena, headquartering at the north end of the canyon, that had been chartered by the first territorial legislature."

Malcolm, a member of the American Fur Trading Company, was "adopted into the Blackfeet tribe," but after the company's relationship with the Blackfeet turned increasingly unstable, he "was later killed in a horse stealing raid, near Helena by Indians." Malcolm was purportedly killed by Mountain Chief's son, and in the attack, Horace, John's father, was left for dead.

John's mother, Margaret, was "a full-blooded Blackfeet," known as First Kill, the daughter of Blackfeet Chief Stands Alone. First Kill, who was born in 1849 and died in 1940, married Horace Clarke in about 1876.

When John was 2, he was afflicted with deafness, most likely the result of a near fatal bout of scarlet fever. Because of this, he never learned language. Despite this trauma, or because of it, Clarke developed strong artistic proclivities, fashioning clay animals that he would present as gifts to his relatives. Struck by the uncanny likenesses of these creations, Margaret encouraged her son to amble the mud banks near his home to gather more clay. She also instructed him to be quick to observe wildlife, but methodical in examining it, instilling in the boy a sense of accuracy in shape and form not teachable in art schools or in books. Perhaps, even then, Margaret recognized that art would be Clarke's source of understanding and compassion, his refuge.

Clarke lived in Highwood until he was 7, when his father sold the family ranch. Around this time, his family members and elders, recognizing the permanence of the young boy's lack of communication, named him Ca-ta-pu-ie, meaning Man-Who-Talks-Not. The same year the family moved to the Sweet Grass Hills, where his father "cultivated sheep and mining interests."

Taught to read and write at Fort Shaw Indian School, Clarke was sent to a series of schools for the deaf, including periods at the North Dakota School for the Deaf at Devil's Elbow from 1894 to 1897 and the Montana School for the Deaf and Blind at Boulder (the school is now at Great Falls) from 1898 to 1899. At one such school, St. John's School for the Deaf in Milwaukee, Wisconsin, Clarke was introduced to woodcarving through a vocational training course in furniture decoration. During the course, it was said that he excelled in altar carving. He must have impressed somebody in Milwaukee with his ability because he was asked to carve church alters in that city.

East Glacier Studio

THE CLARKE FAMILY eventually moved to the community of Midvale, most likely in 1913, which later became East Glacier, "where they had a land grant north of the Great Northern Railway tracks and where the Glacier Park Hotel now stands," according to one account of the area's history.

The mass and extent of the fledgling park—it was established as America's 10th national park just three years earlier, in May 1910—was a great benefit to John Clarke, providing the backdrop of observation and inspiration to live his art wholeheartedly. It would not have been unusual to see Clarke hunting or fishing or traveling around East Glacier in his Jeep on the search for burls, weather-beaten roots and twisted pieces of lakeshore wood.

Clarke's studio was a scene from the animal kingdom, from bears to horses, to buffalo and mountain goats. Soft, spongy cottonwood, though difficult to carve, was his favored medium of wood; its suppleness allowed Clarke to rough the fibers into realistically shaggy animal fur. He commonly used heavy bark, cedar, walnut and maple, too. Not limited to carving, Clarke also addressed the world in crayon and painted in oil.

Clarke worked through the long winters under the sway of the park's soothing, yet severe, beauty. Living simply with few possessions, he kept his body healthy. Under the golden thaw of sunshine, he would exhibit his art outside, in full display of the tourists who often lined the perimeter of the small studio. With dark eyes peering through his glasses, he would chisel for them a reproduction of his favorite puppy, from the trunk of a tree that he had chopped down on the mountainside.

Lamp carvings on desks in the big hotels and the little animals for sale in their novelty shops would have been identifiable to locals as Clarke's work. His first exhibition outside of the area was held in Helena in 1916. Among the pieces exhibited was a bison bull and cow, which through a long string of events commanded the attention of someone associated with an esteemed sculpture school in New York. According to a 1933 edition of True West, "Critics, artists and gallery conductors from the east came to the park, saw what he was doing and encouraged him."

His reputation as a sculptor accrued due to his ability to depict the animals of the wild with realistic accuracy. He traveled around to work at fairs and made his living solely from his art, selling pieces that ranged from five to five hundred dollars.

Though unable to correspond through sound—"deaf and dumb," "deaf Indian" or "deaf and mute" are written descriptions that commonly prefaced the artist—Clarke was very responsive to people, communicating with the same pencils and pads that he used for sketching.

"John liked people very much, and they liked him," said artist Bob Morgan, in a radio program that aired in February, 1972, about Clarke titled "The Man Who Speaks Not." "Why, there were people who went back to East Glacier year after year just to see John Clarke. And he had a special way to reply when someone wrote to see when their work would be completed. He would send a post card, on which was sketched the work in its present state. It might show a half-finished figure, or even a Jeep heading out over the country to take the artist where he could observe wildlife."

A Revered Sculptor

CLARKE WAS CONSIDERED a great sculptor because of his afore-mentioned keen perception of wildlife, his long hours of observation of the animals in their true habitat, his superior anatomical precision, and his meticulous practice in depicting them in their natural poses. "His figures are correct to the finest detail and his work, like that of western artists, is a definite contribution to posterity," trumpeted the *Great Falls Tribune* in 1932.

Indeed, President Warren G. Harding owned an eagle holding an American flag carved by Clarke, which was displayed in the White House. Business magnate John D. Rockefeller purchased four of his carvings in 1924 alone. A visit from Charles M. Russell (1864-1926) to Clarke's studio was an annual summer occurrence for many years, until ill health made it impossible for the prestigious landscape and bronze artist to visit. According to a newsletter published by the Montana School for the Deaf and the Blind in 1927, Russell's arrival "gave the deaf-mute new vision, for there was always friendly, helpful criticisms," while courage was "born anew" in Clarke's heart "for Russell never overlooked good points nor forgot to mention them."

In 1918, Clarke married a woman named Mary Peters and they adopted a daughter, Joyce, in 1931. The family lived in the back of his studio. A writer from the Glacier Reporter described Clarke's home and studio as "old and decrepit."

"John sits on the front porch on the warmer days smoking his pipe and gazing at the Rocky Mountains in the distance," according to the *Glacier Reporter* story. "The porch is laden with twisted and gnarled tree stumps and branches which the old Indian carves into beautiful mountain settings."

In 1940, Clarke was commissioned to deliver two relief panels in wood for the entrance to the Museum of the Plains Indians and Crafts Center in Browning. It's difficult to say how many pieces he completed in his lifetime and how many of them have endured. It has been written that Clarke's works number in the thousands, but no official tally or log has even been conducted.

Nevertheless, late in his eighth decade, he could still be found many hours a day hunched over his work bench in his cabin, whittling bears and mountain goats, his graying hair flopped and split on his deeply etched forehead while his ripened, muscular hands maneuvered back and forth with the carving tools. When not immersed in art, he could be found "beautifully seated, peaceful and smiling," according to the recollection of one visitor.

Working up until his death, Clarke's final months were punctuated by moments of extreme physical discomfort: almost blind, his eyes were so clouded with cataracts that he was unable to discern much beyond indistinct silhouettes. His final known production—a carving of a large grizzly springing itself out of a bear trap—was carried out with the primal touch of awareness and harmony.

Pronounced dead at 4:30 a.m. on November 20, 1970, in Cut Bank Memorial Hospital at age 89, John Louis Clarke was laid to rest in East Glacier Cemetery, in his beloved Glacier National Park.

While his studio was demolished years ago, his work lived on at the John L. Clarke Western Art Gallery & Memorial Museum, established in 1977 in East Glacier, where his art continues to articulate the essence of his voice.

Johnny Breum

(1881-1981)

Postmaster-Fiddler-Photographer Captured
Eastern Montana Through His Eyes

SEVERAL YEARS AGO, the negatives of the photographic jaunts of John Lawrence Breum (1881-1981) were discovered by his descendants in a shoebox roofed in dust. Illustrating his home-town of Fallon, nearby Terry, and the adjoining Badlands, Johnny's photos, which include a self-portrait purportedly from 1902, linger largely unseen. While many of them have yet to even be processed or digitized, approximately 70 of these pictures—an assembly of striking representations of eastern Montana in the early 1900s—are on display at the Prairie County Museum, in Terry.

Indeed, Breum's visuals of the settlers, pioneers, and the mysterious adventures that somehow descended on the plains and its adjacent Badlands are not just visually stunning but significantly enlightening. Preserved in sharp feature, there are images of a load of XIT horses crossing the Yellowstone on Ed Weisner's ferry, headed to Cottonwood Grove, as well as pictures of a group of picnickers crossing the very same wide river mouth. There is an image of a pair of dapper barkeeps and brewmasters positioned in the front of a tavern advertis-ing "Golden Grain Belt Beers," located somewhere between Fallon and the Stockyard. There are cowboys in white sheep-skin chaps ready for work, or taking a breather, or unwinding at chow time. While many of the facts about the subjects, as well as the minutiae of the dates, locations and places of the

picture archive, have been lost to history, there are a number of exciting known facts to be shared about the photographer and the experiences of his vivid life.

An Orphan Who Ended Up in Fallon

JOHN LAWRENCE BREUM was born in Ord, Nebraska, on January 13, 1881, of Norwegian parents, Gunilda and Louis Breum. The Breum family homesteaded at Taylor, North Dakota in 1883, where Louis homesteaded. John was orphaned at five years old, and he and his seven siblings were split into different families. Before he was a teenager, he was in eastern Montana, employed as a trail hand, herding packs of horses originating from North Dakota.

John came to Fallon, then a section of Custer County, with his brother Herman and wife in 1893. According to journals on file at the Prairie County Historical Society, "Johnny had heard stories of sidewalks and bright lights. Actually, they got off at Conlin in the tall weeds and saw only a section house. A friend rowed them across the Yellowstone River in a rowboat."

During the winter of 1894 he attended a one room school in Terry, working for his room and board in the Jordan Hotel.

In 1895 Fallon was said to be not too much more than mud and earth and "a section house or two." It has been said that around that time a man named Al Smith built the first store in Fallon of logs cut and hewn by hand. Another man named Charles Hanson opened another store about 1887.

According to the Breum family journals, John, an avid gardener and hunter, registered to vote in 1902. The registrar was Mr. Brubaker who later opened the Terry Bank, and he never missed a presidential election. John carried out ranch work for John Van for several years. "At this time there were huge stockyards in Fallon where the elevators now stand, the wings extended a quarter mile across the flat. Fallon was then the largest cattle shipping point in the northwest."

Varied Life: Postmaster, Fiddler, and Photographer

In 1908, "Johnny," as he was known to his family and friends, was appointed Fallon postmaster, a post he held until around 1914. Not unusual considering the period, the post office was located in his home. According to one contemporary newspaper account, "One day a man came in and asked for a draft, and got angry when told there was no such thing as a postal draft. But since he insisted, John opened a door and a window and asked him to stand between, and said, that was the only draft he'd ever get there. Threatening to report the postmaster, the man took his complaint to the depot and purchased an express money order."

John and Clara Weisner, a Fallon resident, the daughter of South Dakota homesteaders, were married in 1919. Their two children, Cliff and Fern, were born in Fallon, in 1920 and 1922, respectively.

Some of John's hobbies were common ones, including setting lines for catfish in the Yellowstone River. Early in the morning he would check on the lines, remove the fish, if any, and re-bait. His other hobbies were more nuanced. When he was 17 or 18, he played violin for dances in the Fallon area. He would travel to the local ranches on horseback with his violin strapped to his back. The plan would be to arrive at the ranch in time for supper, where many neighbors would be gathered for the dance. He and his fellow musicians loved to perform and socialize, so much so that the conviviality would sometimes extend from sunset to sunrise, and two days or more elapsed at breakneck speed. Johnny's account describes the average occasion as an evening of music and dancing and then a rest for a midnight supper, before the music and dancing reignited and grooved straight through daylight. Only after breakfast was served would the musicians agree that it was time to be headed on their way home. As far as recompense, he noted that "a hat was passed for the music."

He was a member of the Terry Montana Corn Belt band which formed in 1909 and re-formed in 1915. Breum and his ragtag pack of cohorts traveled to the Black Hills of South Dakota in 1927 to present President Calvin Coolidge a pair of chaps and perform at a celebration of his birthday. There were 70 people in the party, including John and Clara, who did the cooking for the crowd. The couple made the nearly three-hundred-mile trip in a Model T Coupe, part of a caravan of 22 cars. At one point, Johnny owned a 24-passenger school bus which he purchased and drove back to Fallon from

Lima, Ohio. For many years, he transported Fallon youngsters, including his own children, to Terry High School.

Documented Railroads to Ranches

IN ADDITION TO BEING A CATTLE RANCHER and a fiddler, Johnny, as it turned out, was an early incarnation of the documentary photographer, depicting things such as cowboys on the ferry, at the sleeping tent, and at the bunkhouse, as well as the nature of ranching roundups and calf brandings. Through the scope and extent of Johnny's camera, we see sheep grazing near the headwaters of Cabin Creek and the men in primitive-looking machinery harvesting wheat in Fallon Flats in 1908, as well as XIT cattle obediently fording the Yellowstone River.

About 1907 Johnny was traversing the earth on a horse and buggy and taking pictures of ranches and businesses and such developments throughout the country, including the novel expansion of the Milwaukee Railroad. When the Milwaukee Railroad inaugurated activity through the Fallon area at about this time, 1906-1907, Johnny was there to preserve images of the required digging, clearing, and construction. Perceptive to the archival and commercial nature of his photography, he even sold some of the images to the company and the crew. One existing photo, taken on the 4th of July, undated, depicts the Northern Pacific Bridge over Fallon Creek.

While no record exists as to the basis of Johnny's initial introduction to photography, in one written account he noted that he used a camera with glass plates, 6 x 8, fixed on a tripod. South of the Fallon depot, he had built a tar papered shack with a stove pipe for a chimney where he lived and developed his pictures.

Breum's photography exposes his passion for the surrounding Badlands, their curious table top rock formations, and their irregular (and seemingly endless) craggy nooks and stony alcoves, places that he labeled with names such as the Balanced Rocks, the Lion's Lookout, the Hole in the Wall, and the National Bridge. Some of Johnny's available photos include Custer's Pillar near Glendive, Indian Creek Rock, north of Fallon, and a mammoth ice barge on the Yellowstone River.

Despite his evident affinity for this special territory, Johnny Breum and family moved from Fallon to Seattle in 1948, and he died in Washington State in 1981. Several years ago, Terri Smith, a friend of Johnny Breum's granddaughter, Cheryl Breum, contacted the Prairie County Museum about the surprising discovery of his photography collection, an unorganized assortment of negatives said to be found in a small cardboard shoebox. Approximately 70 of them were eventually developed and then later compiled and self-printed in a thick portfolio booklet by Terri and Cheryl. Some of these booklets were donated to the Prairie County Museum, in Terry, perhaps not coincidentally, home to a pair of galleries celebrating the much greater-known work of pioneer photographer Evelyn Cameron (1868-1928).

George Lowry

(1886-1965)

Dirigible Balloonist Sailing the Big Sky

From the exhibition jumps at the Helena Fair and at the Spokane Fair in 1911, to the inflatable dirigible balloon he sailed over Butte in 1914, George Lowry was no doubt a spectacular showman and theatrical spirit.

While the average person gazed at the sky with their feet firmly and safely planted on the ground—and was content to keep it that way—Lowry wondrously pointed to the clouds convincing himself that that was where he needed to be. Indeed, he crossed two of Montana's high passes before the days of powered flight—descending the Continental Divide by parachute several miles east of Butte and carried by the wind across the Bozeman pass, landing east.

In an act that would have even made legendary showman P.T. Barnum chuckle, he once parachuted with a team of monkeys, and another time he released white leghorn chickens from high in the air of a dirigible balloon, with prize tags attached. Lowry said that enjoyed both the balloon ride and the general excitement of his trips with the animals; he noted that the chickens and the monkeys seemed to enjoy their ascents and plunges, too.

Transfixed By Paper Balloon, Aeronautics

George Lowry was born on January 11, 1886 at Homestake, Montana, his first years spent in a log boarding house. His

parents later shifted to Butte, where, according to Lowry's own account, he became transfixed with a Chinese paper balloon he was given as a kid, and this object sparked a lifelong interest in aeronautics.

In 1908 Lowry purchased his first balloon and parachute from a Chicago balloon company that at full inflation swelled to 85 feet in height and measured 65 feet through the bulge. The muslin structured balloon was part of a full package—instructions, parachute and trapeze—at a cost of $175. A reference to an unsuccessful flight attempt by Lowry during the celebration on the Fourth of July in Basin in 1908 appeared in the *Basin Progress* and *Mining Review*. Heavy wind disrupted the afternoon balloon ascension and Lowry narrowly missed a serious accident, falling 20 feet, and injuring his wrist. The balloon caught fire and floated over the city, before landing onto the roof of a bake oven and being put out. Alas, the badly burned balloon prompted Lowry to cancel the evening performance.

Lowry owned at least three balloons during the time between 1908 and 1917 when he toured the country making exhibition flights. He made repeat engagements in a number of Montana cities and annually followed a fair circuit in the Midwest, which included stops at Minot, North Dakota; Davenport, Iowa; Rock Island; and Chicago, Illinois. In one interview, Lowry claimed that he had inherent fear of water because he never learned how to swim, and it was only after considerable persuasion that he agreed to make an exhibition jump in Chicago, near the shores of Lake Michigan, for Carl McGuire in 1912. Lowry received for this jump $150 plus all expenses ($100 in 1912 is worth $2,711.48 today), and he was presented with a fine gold watch engraved by a well-known Chicago jeweler named C.D. Peacock, reading: "Northwest Balloon Association; Chicago, Illinois; 1912; George Lowry."

Quests and Crashes

GEORGE LOWRY CONTINUED EXHIBITION balloon exploits for a number of years. The 1914 Butte City Directory lists him as "a carman for the Butte-street-railway company," and an article in the *Butte Miner*, June 15, 1914, detailed another successful ascension by Lowry, who attained a height of 5,000 feet or more in flight from Lake Avoca. (A man-made lake located on the Flats, Lake Avoca is no longer extant.) The Butte Miners' Union Hall was blown up on the night of June 13-14, 1914, and there was a labor riot at the Miner's Union Day Parades, and that tumult halted many gatherings—but not Lowry's.

While the weather was reported to be "threatening," he was not taken off course by wind and remained in the air approximately 20 minutes, "long enough to give the big crowd of spectators a most interesting exhibition." The *Butte Miner* noted that Lowry was "making quite a success as an aeronaut" and that he "intended to devote his entire time to this somewhat dangerous but thrilling occupation."

In 1915 he purchased a dirigible balloon in Columbus, Montana, which had been manufactured in Frankfort, New York, by inventor and meteorologist Carl E. Myers. On his first attempt to inflate the dirigible in Butte the generator exploded, injuring several spectators and landing Lowry in the hospital for several months, partially blinded by fragments of steel and shrapnel in both eyes.

With his vision diminished and body ragged, Lowry once again returned to the thrill of the skies, making his final balloon ascension in Deer Lodge in 1926. The perennial showman, he didn't want to give up aeronautics, but he did so at the urging of his wife. After many years of balloon voyaging, at age 40 he mundanely started another career as an electrician at the Montana Power Company. Lowry died in Butte in January of 1965 at the age of 79.

Pintsize Powerhouse Brownie Burke

(1893-1931)

Mascot, Soldier, Thespian Frank J. "Brownie" Burke

WHEN THE UNITED STATES entered World War I in April 1917, Frank J. Burke, a major league baseball mascot, repeatedly but unsuccessfully tried to join the American Expeditionary Forces. "A perfectly formed midget," according to one description, Burke, nicknamed "Brownie," stood between 4'3" and 4'7" (accounts vary), weighed 90 lbs. Undeterred, Brownie pressed on, eventually wearing a doughboy's uniform, earning the rank of corporal, and seeing duty on the Continent.

Born at Marysville, Montana, on May 19, 1893, Frank J. Burke was the fourth of eight children of a carpenter. He grew up amid a gold and silver boom there and later in Helena. Diminutive size propelled him into becoming a drum leader and, in tune with the times, mascot and batboy for Helena-area baseball teams. "I mascotted the Helena team in the Inter-mountain league and they won 25 out of 27 games they played before the league was busted up," he said years later.

He played shortstop; the April 29, 1907, *Helena Independent-Record* describes him as the area's leading batter and fielder at that position. "Brownie is 40 inches high, weighs 40 pounds, bats .440 and fields .940," the paper wrote. "Baseball must be his forte."

Around 1909, Burke found work as a bellhop at the Mammoth Hot Springs hotel at Yellowstone National Park.

En route home from Los Angeles, California, August Herrmann, owner of the Cincinnati Reds baseball team, stayed at the Mammoth. Encountering young Burke, the team owner found him "an intelligent and well-read person," wrote the *Pittsburgh Daily Post* on April 29, 1912. Herrmann asked the youth to be the Reds  mascot; after consulting his mother, Brownie, 16, signed on. In Cincinnati and on the road, he performed pantomimes and comic routines to entertain fans, interrupting his antics to chase stray balls for umpires and collect bats for players. He sent his salary, a sum, he once said, considerably over his thirty-five dollars a month in bell-boy wages, home, in part to help one of his sisters study music. "The highest salaried mascot in the business," the August 6, 1909 *Knoxville Sentinel* said of him.

During his six years with the Reds, he accepted an invitation from the Orpheum Stock Company to join that vaudeville troupe. When not on the diamond or in the dugout he trod the boards on the B.F. Keith circuit, whose theaters dotted the big cities of the East Coast. Along with playing children, he filled roles that included Buster Brown, mascot of the Brown Shoe Company, and "a dunce" in a popular Maude Adams play, "Quality Street."In October1913, Burke, with ballplayers, team managers like Clarke Griffith of the Washington Senators, and other baseball figures, called on President Woodrow Wilson White House at the president's country retreat in Cornish, New Hampshire. "He sure is a fine guy," Burke said of Wilson.

With the country's entry into war Burke's ambitions drastically changed. According to the May 10, 1918, *Salt Lake Telegram*, his relentless pursuit of military service led General Henry T. Allen, commander of the U.S. Army's 90th Division, to instruct examining officers to overlook Burke's size. He was sworn in and at first assigned a clerical position. He was enlisted into the Ninetieth Infantry Division, Headquarters Detachment, on June 1, 1918, according to *the Billings Gazette*, July 27, 1919, within weeks landed at Le Havre, trained at Ain-Le-Duc and Cote d'Or, near Dijon, and went into battle in the St. Mihiel sector, and later in the Meuse-Argonne offensive, one the largest and deadline actions in American military operations. FYI: War department records say that Brownie served overseas from June 21, 1918 to June 7, 1919.

Brownie served for 13 months in France and the Army of Occupation in Germany—12 of them as a corporal in the headquarters detachment of the 90th Division, which was on the battle line for 78 days (*Billings Gazette*, July 27, 1919). "Every soldier and the Germans in Berncastle knew this fellow," American Legion magazine wrote in a 1940 article. He was honorably discharged on June 18, 1919.

Brownie moved to California in 1921, where he continued his acting career and affiliation with baseball. His final season in baseball, 1927, he managed the Martinsburg, West Virginia, Blue Sox, a Class D club in the Blue Ridge League. He died suddenly in Bakersfield, California, on November 7, 1931, of a lung disorder. He was 38.

Maria Montana

(1893-1971)

Lewistown Songbird Who Scored
in Grand Opera

"To start at the beginning, I should explain that I grew up in a small western town where music was almost a myth and living was pretty strait-laced and a young aspirant had small chance to look on varied life—which is one of the things a singer should do to broaden her spirit for music."

And so begins the tale of opera star "Maria Montana," or "Marie Montana," born Ruth Kellogg Waite, who was about 33 years old at the time of the quote, and had already won a wide reputation at home and abroad as a soprano opera singer.

Persistence and hard work served as the Lewistown girl's education and subsequently paved the path to a splendid success in her chosen love. The one-time telephone operator had struggled to get a musical education, though she used every local resource imaginable and somehow developed a reputation as a talent.

Indeed, eventually singing in Italy, the home of grand opera, the "Lewistown Songbird" scored success after success, a harbinger of things to come across Europe and elsewhere.

Daughter of United States Marshal

BORN ON JANUARY 23, 1893, in Wallace, Idaho, Ruth's grandfather was a "forty-niner" in the California gold rush days and her grandmother was a San Francisco girl. She was the

 second oldest child of John "Jack" Kellogg Waite and Alice May Bunyard. Jack was prone to fisticuffs and brawling, once having his skull cracked in a fracas with six Salt Lake City policemen. After surviving a frighteningly near fatal avalanche, Jack packed up the Waite family and, perhaps ironically, joined a sheriff department in Montana. (While records are hazy and the timeline is at times hard to straighten out, both Butte and Helena later claimed a hometown connection to Ruth and her family.)

According to one account, White was widely known in Butte and the Northwest "in the old days" as an athlete—the *Butte Miner* said that he was "the old camp's most famous athlete"—and, retaining an apparent blood lust for fighting, once came near defeating heavyweight pugilist John L. Sullivan in a "memorable" ring encounter in the Butte mining camp.

He was made a deputy under United States Marshal for the District of Montana, William McDermott, a presidential appointee, whose term lasted from 1894- 1898.

Jack later prospected and partnered with Archibald E. Spriggs, who served as the lieutenant governor of Montana from 1897 to 1901, on a copper mine. Jack was at one time said to be associated with pioneer mining man and U.S. Senator W.A. Clark.

Jack Waite died in Helena February 18, 1902. According to contemporary accounts, White's "official duties" took him to a dingy back room in a saloon in the "mining quarter" of Helena. Shots rang out, and one of the first people to reach the scene was a newspaper reporter. There on a card table sprawled the lifeless body of Waite, "in his hand was a smoking Colt revolver." Apparently, the reporter "immediately" drove to the outskirts of the city to notify the widow of the dead man, and perhaps score a few raw quotes. A second account, however, says that he lived for an additional 12 hours after he was shot, so the timeline of the incident isn't altogether clear.

The newspaper reporter was "confronted by a pretty woman with a babe in her arms and three little tots holding to her skirts," it was written in the first telling. One of these orphaned children was Ruth.

One theory for the motive of death put forward that someone whose hatred for Waite had "incurred through performance of his duty" as a U.S. marshal had "drawn faster" than he. But subsequent reports rejected that he was killed in the line of duty, or even killed by another period, and the single shot from the .44 to the right temple of his head was determined to have been a self-inflicted wound.

Ruth then moved with her family to Lewistown, but only a "cow camp on the plains," as she later recalled it.

Debuts, Develops As Singer

BEGINNING IN HER TEENS, she was the musical pride of Lewistown and in big demand for weddings, funerals and public functions. Her debut as a soloist was in a production of The Mikado, in January 1906, when she was 13-years old.

In May, 1906, she participated in a fundraiser for St. Mary's School of Lewistown, giving the recitation, performing in a pantomime skit, and singing at the graduation ceremony. She also performed at that year's town July 4 celebrations. In late 1907 she sang at the Bijou Theater in Lewistown, and the following spring was in a concert supporting role and then returned to the Bijou in May. She sang again in the fall, putting a clever twist on Kate Vannah's *Good Bye, Sweet Day!* In 1909 she won a piano in a newspaper subscription contest and sang in concerts in September and November.

The 1910 United States Census places her and several siblings in the household of Alice Waite, living in Lewistown. Alice was without a job, but the oldest sibling Edward was employed as a bookkeeper and Ruth was listed as a telephone operator. That year she was first dubbed in print as the "Lewistown songbird," routinely performing at local weddings, baby showers, and community events. It is not known how long she worked as a telephone operator.

Ruth relished the cultural exchange of the arts and often joined traveling artists in their local performances. Slowly, Ruth expanded into Great Falls with performances and plays.

Soprano Star

AT 20 YEARS OLD, she learned that she was accepted into the Toronto Conservatory of Music (later renamed the Royal Conservatory) and departed in 1914. She received the artist's degree after only two years of study.

Studying under Ernestina Bruschini, her music rise was noticeably swift. She was in demand all over Italy and finally reached the most famous of all of the Italian opera houses, the San Carlo opera house of Naples, where she performed as Gilda in "Rigoletto." Soon, she was recognized as an artist of ability, having an excellent voice, intellectual background, and pleasing personality.

She intended to sing under her own name, but the bland, monosyllabic "Waite" seemed difficult to the Italians; the word Montana handled easily in a non-English speaking tongue and apparently made things a bit smoother sailing for Ruth in foreign countries and the moniker "Maria Montana" or "Marie Montana" contributed much to recognition.

To say that Ruth was a world-famous soprano singer is a bit of an undervaluation. Indeed, the young singer was given a great ovation and quickly demonstrated that she merited all the praise. Across the continent of Europe there was virtually no venue she didn't perform at or no operative occasion that she wasn't invited to. Indeed, discriminating European audiences encored her repeatedly. She "registered beautiful achievements" not just in Italy and France, but China and Canada and the U.S. At Naples, Italy, Princess Xenia of Greece was so favorably impressed by Maria's voice that she selected her to sing at the wedding of the princess to William B. Leeds, Jr., the son of an American businessman who dominated the tin plate industry.

She returned to Lewistown in the summer of 1916, where an audience packed the Judith Theater to welcome her home. She worked as a soloist with the New York Philharmonic, the Chicago, Cleveland, and St. Louis symphonies, and other prominent musical organizations. At the Stadium Concerts in New York, she was soloist under Dutch conductor Willem van Hoogstraten.

When she made her debut in 1927 in New York in a recital at the Town Hall, the critic of the *New York Sun* said "Maria Montana, soprano, gave one of the best song recitals of the season. She disclosed a beautiful voice; she used it with skill, and her general style was that of a singer to the manner born."

In the *San Francisco Call-Bulletin* praise was expressed by one critic who observed at Ruth's debut concert with the San

Francisco Symphony in front of "a great crowd of 10,000 people" that "she has a distinguished stage manner and is young and comely. Her training is patently Italian."

Throughout the Great Depression, Ruth was able to find steady employment in the arts and performed at concert halls and on radio stations nationwide. She returned to Montana frequently to teach, to sing, to socialize, and to fundraise and perform. Indeed, newspaper clippings are chock-full of sightings: a visit to a church in Hardin; a fundraiser at the Lions Club in Great Falls; a talk at the Lewistown Rotary Club; a class study on Faust; a reception here and a recital there; concerts for assorted Moose Lodges.

Ruth continually remained active in the opera world straight through the late-1960s, either as a teacher and lecturer, a program director, or as talent.

She died at age 78 of injuries suffered in an automobile accident, in La Jolla, California, in 1971. Perhaps the final words about "Maria Montana" should be the ones planted by an admiring journalist in California, who, in 1935, wrote this of the Fergus County girl whose "fresh charm of voice" pleased the world with songs:

"Here is a young American singer over whom hovers the mantle of authentic greatness."

MERRILL K. RIDDICK

(1895-1988)

Perennial Losing Candidate for Public Office

CERTAINLY, MERRILL K. RIDDICK was a print from which there was no other negative.

He theorized and proposed a new science as a solution to problems of pollution control and water reuse. Thrilled by aviation as a young boy, he performed aeronautical stunts at circuses with Charles A. Lindbergh. And despite the certainty of losing, he ran three utterly out-of-the-ordinary Presidential campaigns, traveling on the seats of a string of Greyhound buses.

Born in Wisconsin on March 7, 1895, Merrill moved to Fergus County, Montana with his family at about age 15. His father, Carl W. Riddick, a newspaperman and wheat and cattle rancher, represented eastern Montana in Congress twice, in 1919 and 1921. Carl left office after being defeated by Burton K. Wheeler in the 1922 U.S. Senate Race.

As a teenager and young adult, Merrill vagabonded across the Pacific Northwest and the West, mesmerized by the skill of pilots and the vigor of planes. He graduated at the Army Air Force Aeronautics School in San Diego in 1917, flew reconnaissance planes over Europe in the First World War, and was one of the Post Office's first airmail pilots, operating the airmail between New York and Washington.

Eventually, Riddick tendered his resignation as an air mail pilot. Throughout the 1920s, he earned his paycheck presented plane rides to the public at county fairs, or barnstorming, touring rural lands to provide aerial performances, often originating or conclud-

ing in barns. In 1924, he gave a ride to a young woman in Kentucky; they were engaged the next day.

In 1928, he worked at the nation's first private aviation school, Embry-Riddle Aeronautical University, and around that time formed a friendship with the famous World War I fighter pilot Eddie Rickenbacker. Riddick graduated as an airplane pilot from the Austin School of Military Aeronautics and became an aviation instructor and technical inspector of planes during World War II.

Somehow, he ended up in Philipsburg, Montana perhaps because of his interest in gold prospecting. It was in these years that Riddick became a scientist of sorts, a philosopher and perennial candidate for public office.

Birth of a Theory

MERRILL RIDDICK PROPOSED a new science that he called "Applied Human Ecology." He pamphleteered with typed and photocopied pages of discursive, though salient, theories, and printed hundreds of copies of journal editions discussing them. Environmental control required striking a balance between pollution (a word he frequently spelled with only one letter l) and the development of our natural resources. Half as long would have been twice as good. Riddick was verbose, and his manifestos were as dense as marsh thickets in the Pint-

lars, Riddick's manifestos were noted for the tangential. But that's not to say that he was out of step with reality. Indeed, his papers confirm him as an early seeker after ecological truth, a purveyor of "the need of human adjustment to new modes of dealing with the complicated factors and variables" of environmental control.

He was determined to promote his progressive ideas in earnest. For Riddick, Montana was a live test, a laboratory experiment in the making. Trudging off into the political wilderness, Riddick launch his aspirations with a quest for the Montana Democratic gubernatorial nomination in 1960.

By and large, Riddick believed that the solution to a crisis required not ideological but pragmatic solutions. According to material written, circulated and paid for by Riddick to promote his candidacies for governor of Montana, he would use the position as a platform of natural resource potential development. Here are the five key tenets of Riddick's platform as he set them out.

1. A barge canal up the Missouri River into Montana as far as Fort Benton.
2. A barge canal up the Milk River into Canada.
3. Water to put into the Snake River for the proposed 515-mile aqueduct from the Snake River to Lake Mead (just about Hoover Dam) on the Colorado River.
4. Compensation for Canada for additional water that will drown out the Pick-Sloan controversy (conflict between the Buerau (sic) of Reclamation and U.S. Army Engineers, that has resulted in committing water in the Missouri 4 ½ times its content) and stopping the Dakotas from getting Montana to sell her birthright for lower Missouri river basin development.
5. The down-river demands are the biggest piracy of Montana rights in history.

He finished last in a field of six, receiving about 1,000 votes. He decided to launch a second bid for the same office in 1968. Same result: few votes, last place among six Democrats.

His candidacies for political office now little more than a formality, he decided to switch parties. His career as a Republican was similarly ill-fated. In a field of four Republicans vying for the U.S. Senate in 1972, he came in fourth, receiving around 1,500 votes.

Puritan Ethic and Epic, Magnetohydrodynamics, and Prohibition Party

UNDETERRED BY THE SENATE LOSS, or perhaps perversely motivated by it, he then "raised the ante" and started his own tongue-knotting presidential ticket: the Puritan Ethic and Epic, Magnetohydrodynamics, and Prohibition Party. Magnetohydrodynamics, according to Britannica, is the description of the behavior of a plasma," or, in more general terms, "any electrically conducting fluid in the presence of electric and magnetic fields."

The Prohibition component of the title was a double entendre: Riddick saw political fundraising as congenitally dishonest and unfair and he campaigned on the pledge to bar not just alcohol, which, in his estimate, was an incorrigibly sordid problem, but also illegal campaign contributions. He would, however, innocuously accept donations of a single dollar or less.

Riddick first ran for the White House in 1976, paying for mailers with military pension checks. Using his post office box in Philipsburg as the correspondence address, Riddick described himself in one handbill as "a widower-pensioner, 3 children, 10 grandchildren, veteran of WW1 and WW2 and half a century of reserve service—not addicted to dope or alcohol."

Here's one advertisement that Riddick ran in a Montana newspaper:

"Merrill Riddick for President (no political contributions accepted). There are many ways to solve the energy crisis, besides giving a monopoly to the folks who bribe enough politicians. These would include: (1) Solar Energy, (2) Thermal Energy, (3) Ocean Energy, (4) Hydrocarbon use."

Days after Jimmie Carter was elected president of the United States in 1976, Riddick affirmed his intention to run once again in 1980. He also ran for president in 1984. All three times he nominally campaigned across the country on the Greyhound buses where he also lived and slept. Two-month unrestricted bus passes, he said, were economically expedient. Instead of posting up in a hotel, "for less than $12 a day," the Social Security recipient told the media, he could live on the bus.

"Evel Knievel" as Veep?

LARGELY SYMBOLIC, these candidacies had been virtually ignored by the mainstream press outside of Montana, whereas reporters and photographers almost always outnumbered supporters at his events in the state. Once, after the car caravan that Riddick had counted on to promote his candidacy in Missoula failed to materialize, he merely hopped back onto the bus and returned home to Philipsburg.

During his first presidential candidacy, Riddick announced that an artist from Coos Bay, Oregon named "Lim Bow" would be his vice president (this name was a lark, perhaps a silly variant of the word *limbo*). Within weeks, Riddick said that he rescinded the offer to Lim Bow, something that he drolly attributed to "a philosophical disagreement on the nature of campaign conduct."

Mindful of the attention derived through odd self-promotion, he then proffered the name of superstar daredevil Robert Craig "Evel" Knievel as a possibility to fill the vacancy. Riddick ostensibly hoped to exploit the Butte native's gargantuan celebrity—and his presumably indignant rebuff—as a springboard to boost his own campaign. Nominally the VP nominee, Knievel never accepted the bestowal, and Riddick later admitted that he was unable to even make contact with him to extend the invitation.

The quick-witted octogenarian, however, always could be counted on to spin a good yarn. Riddick occasionally entertained amused reporters in his small home office, located between a funeral home and the Antler's Bar and Café in downtown Philipsburg.

Crouched at a table cluttered with notebooks, books, boxes, and scraps of political ephemera, he liked to tell stories like this one to captive reporters: according to Riddick, the U.S. government once needed 50,000 airplanes for World War II, so it commenced "a worldwide search for sapphires." The government, then, dug 20 tons of sapphires in Philipsburg and shipped six tons to Switzerland to support the war effort. In Riddick's framing of events, Hitler intercepted the sapphire shipment, and the bulk of the sapphires were returned to Philipsburg.

Riddick was 89 years of age during his final bid for the presidency in 1984, a token so tenuously pursued that Riddick didn't even bother to name a running mate. Tossing his hat in the ring was more sideshow ceremony than serious decorum, yet, in keeping with Riddick's confident public manner for the past 25 years, he was never less than certain of his own integrity and his good intentions.

In February 1987, he moved to Annapolis, Maryland, to live with his sister, Ruth McLain, and soon after needed to be placed at a convalescent center. When he died of cancer on Wednesday, March 9, 1988, the Associated Press noted the unique affection that many people in Montana held for the quirky eccentric.

"Perennial losing candidates are not unusual in American politics. But Riddick's quests earned him a place in the hearts of many in Montana, a state proud of its individualists."

The Riddick Field Airport in Philipsburg was named in 1976, perhaps for both his distinguished aviation career and for his flights of fancy.

MYRON BRINIG

(1896-1991)

The Author Who Hated His Hometown

"THAT'S SILVER BOW FOR YOU," he once wrote in one of his novels about his boyhood town, "One day you got plenty of everything you want, an' the next you're starvin' to death... anything is li'ble to happen in this town."

For all of the nuance of dialogue and stylish arrangement of language that pervades the work of Butte novelist Myron Brinig, for all of the wonderful ways in which he painted a colorful picture of Butte in its raucous adolescence, and for all of the fascinating and revealing conversations and behaviors that he considered, internalized, and later transformed as the basis of his successful vernacular novels, perhaps it is ironic that he so despised the town that he created—and that created him.

Indeed, he made his name novelizing Butte, yet the mention of the great, rich hill made him resentful and angry. The Minneapolis-born Jew wasn't troubled by the town's hostility—indeed, he later recalled a childhood remarkably free of anti-Semitism or class warfare or xenophobia—he was agitated by the radical, pro-proletarian politics of the day, and interpreted the town as "a hard, bitter place," that shunned intellectualism and was smothered by leftist tribalism.

The overpowering theme of his mining town-cum-childhood reminiscences books—he authored 21 novels between 1929 and 1958—became how the town dominated the cultural life of Montana and how it changed people—and not for the better.

Since its earliest hours, Butte has impressed people as a uniquely squalid and mesmerizing place. "The black heart of Montana," was how historian Joseph Kinsey Howard once referred to it; author Mary MacLane resented her having been stuck in such an "uncouth" and "warped" and "ugly" town. Indeed, Brinig's dislike of Butte, while hardly endemic to  him, was most unmistakable, his novels largely judgmental of the city, never dull but always depressing. On the other hand, he owned a restless fascination for Butte and its miners, labor organizers, saloons, and businessmen, and all of the, remained popular literary topics.

Son of a Romanian immigrant and shopkeeper, Myron, the youngest of ten siblings, was born in Minneapolis on Dec. 22, 1896. When he was 3, the family moved to Butte, with records indicating that the family (seven boys, one girl) at one point resided at 814 W. Granite St. The copper metropolis boasted 30,470 inhabitants in 1900, and 39,165 in 1910.

Above all, Butte was frenzied—it never ceased. Myron's father, Maurice "Moses" Brinig, owned a store right around the bend from the red-light district and shabby whorehouses of town, and from a very young age Myron recalled that he and his brothers watched the hectic intensity of "dizzy blondes, bromidic brunettes, [and] rampaging redheads" from "down the line," as the district was generally known.

Wedged in a tight area of several blocks of lean-tos and a congestion of cabins, the notorious district spanned "both sides of Galena street from Main to Wyoming, [the] alley east of Main between Galena and Mercury and Paradise alley from Wyoming west, also Little Terrace..."

Myron attended the McKinley School and the Butte High School. At the age of seventeen, he studied at New York University and later at Columbia University (eventually earning two degrees)—in between serving in the US Army in World War I—and started his career by writing short stories for magazines. He journeyed West in the late 1920s seeking work as a screenplay writer in Hollywood. He worked in an automobile agency, in a motion picture studio, in a shop where paints and lumber were sold and travelled in "semi-hobo" fashion through France, Spain, and England. His first short stories accepted for publication were chiefly about the lives of prize-fighters.

No matter where he resided, he hung on to all of his memories of Silver Bow County and its big city excitement and blight, eventually combining them with his own fresh insights into a series of successful novels, including, most critically, *Singermann* (1929), *Wide Open Town* (1931), *This Man Is My Brother* (1932) and *The Sun Sets in the West* (1935).

Critical Praise of Singermann

HIS FIRST NOVEL *Singermann* (1929) earned winning praise for its vivid depiction of the lives of Butte's Jewish community, the protagonist Singermann inspired by his father, Maurice.

When Myron Brinig was asked if he felt his novel could have been set in the Lower East Side of New York City and elicited the same response, he became annoyed.

"No, no. Not *Singermann*. It couldn't possibly have been

set on the Lower East Side...because the way the people react to their surroundings is much different in the far West than it is on the East Side. There is a different climate, different types of people and a feeling of being a part of a new world which is quite different from the feeling of being on the East Side. You're here in a mountain town surrounded by miners and not many Jewish people and so your reactions are going to be different.'"

The protagonist Singermann was inspired by his father, Maurice Brinig, and a number of phrases and names and references from his childhood undoubtedly informed his work. "Many a young man was seduced away from godliness on Saturday night," wrote Brinig, who in later interviews referred to Butte as a "wide open town." One of Brinig's novels, a luridly colorful epic of Butte in the heyday of copper mining, almost obsessed in its focus on the explicit confluence of frontiersmen, saloons and brothels, was named *Wide Open Town.*

Another Brinig top seller was *The Sisters,* a 1937 family odyssey transformed into a 1938 movie with Bette Davis and Errol Flynn, brilliantly depicting the unique attitudes of bums, whores, and millionaires, in a city housing one of the oddest social orders to be found anywhere. The plot of *The Sisters* covers the four years between the presidential elections of Teddy Roosevelt (1904) and William Howard Taft (1908), and the vigorous relationship between the people of Montana and the age in which they live. The film version's premiere took place in the city that inspired it, with the cast arriving in Butte for its initial presentation.

"For the first time in its history," roared one Butte newspaper, "Butte had an opportunity to observe at close range the buildup, the flag-waving, the press agenting that always accompanies the first presentation of a film play."

As an ascending novelist, Brinig was singled out for his

"artistry and inventiveness in narrative, character and incident," but his later works were dogged by lukewarm reviews
and were even sometimes ridiculed for their "verbosity and
banality." In 1951, *The New York Times Book Review* said his
"sentimental streak and his sympathetic touch with characters
usually lend his books a warm glow of humanity, if not of art."
His tally of novels, include *Madonna Without Child* (1929),
Copper City (1931), *May Flavin* (1938), *Anne Minton's Life*
(1939) and finally *The Looking Glass Heart* (1958).

III-Liberal and Avant Garde

THOUGH HE WAS GAY AND JEWISH, with a calm, quiet exterior,
Brinig could be fierce in print, liberally doling out venomous
stereotypes and much hostility in his works, a hardened, judgmental critic who was not insusceptible to some of the prevail-
ing derisions and prejudices of his era. He wrote disdainfully
of the opium dens of "the Chinks," which though outlawed,
continued to exist in the subterranean passages of the city; he
railed against the dope fiends and the drug addled and the
practitioners of vices such as prostitution, which in his childhood was a normalized occurrence. Native Americans didn't
fare much better than one-dimensional or periphery cutouts, as
Brinig recalled that Indians didn't come to Butte a great deal,
and when they did, it was primarily to cause a ruckus, to fight
and stir trouble, to attain goods or test local whiskey.

Ultimately, Brinig scarcely seemed to recall much that was
pleasant about his childhood in Butte, once emphasizing its
"day to day economic distress, poor health, and overcrowded,
unhealthy, and often impersonal living conditions," which, he
perhaps not so wrongly correlated "to appear to have played a
large part in the number of suicides."

Throughout most of his life, Brining ran in bohemian circles and utopian avant garde groups in New Mexico and New York. He died of gastrointestinal hemorrhage on May 13, 1991, at his home in Manhattan, at 94 years old. Still somewhat of a mystery, either overlooked or only referred to occasionally in fleeting passages as "a completely forgotten writer," his obituary in *The New York Times* accurately describes Brinig as "a novelist most noted for early works recalling the settlement and development."

ALICE GREENOUGH

1902-1995

Rodeo Queen of the West

LONG BEFORE BEN GREENOUGH died in the 1950s, he saw the family surname come to be synonymous with rodeo.

Five of his eight children—Turk, Bill, Frank, Margie, and Alice—went on to the professional rodeo. The family became known as the "Riding Greenoughs." Between them, they most likely captured every championship rodeo to be had. Alice, the first person named to the Cowgirl Hall of Fame, was the most famous of the bunch.

Alice was born in 1902 on a ranch near Red Lodge. Her orphaned father, Ben, arrived in Montana Territory from Illinois via New York City at age 16 in 1884 or 1886 (accounts vary). Ben found work as a cowboy and later mail carrier, at times driving the mail stage from Billings to Red Lodge. He met his wife-to-be on a pack trip while he was selling and breaking horses.

The Greenough family kept dozens of horses to ride, and Alice fed cattle, roped them, and then rounded them up. The open range of the West was Alice's playpen and park. "I can't think of a day in those mountains that we didn't have fun," Alice once recalled.

Alice and her siblings were hardened to withstand a rugged life. "Dad used to leave us in now camps for a month at a time. If we ran out of food, we didn't starve. We killed grouse and ate wild berries. It was the survival of the fittest."

Alice started rodeoing while still in grammar school. "I cut

class to ride saddle broncs in the local fair." When Alice was a teenager, she received her first job, assisting a local rancher who came to the Greenough house looking for hired hands. She and her sister, Marge, also started riding in local rodeos. Alice mostly rode in races, occasionally even bucking broncos. One day Alice and Marge gazed an ad for the "Jack King Wild West Show," which was in need of bronco and trick riders.

Alice won the World's Championship in women's bronc riding in Boston in 1933, '35 and '36 and again in 1940 in New York City. "The saddle bronc event was closed to women after 1941," Alice recalled, because it was said to be "too rough for the girls." The last time Alice took part in the event, only 5 out of 22 women participants didn't end up in the hospital. She and Margie were among them. "It was a hard life, but we could take it," she said, in 1969. "Today's girl would probably fall in a heap."

In 1932 she went to Mexico City to take part in the Rancho Charros, a Mexican fiesta held in the bull ring. "The Mexican people weren't surprised to see a woman bronc rider." She also rode bare back and rode steers. While in Mexico City, she met a Spanish impresario who was contracting bullfighters for a season in Spain. He saw her ride and asked her to go to Spain, where she rodeoed in 40 of that country's largest bull rings.

From Spain, she toured the South of France, and then returned to the U.S. and another season of rodeoing. In a full life of professional rodeoing, Alice traveled throughout the United States, Spain, Mexico, Australia and to Canada. She met the Duke of Windsor while he was still Prince of Wales. "He was a friendly, shy young man," she recalled. Alice met him, and the late King George V and Queen Mary at the royal stables during a trip to England.

In 1934 she again went abroad, this time to England with Tex Austin, a great rodeo producer of that time. Of all the countries she had visited, Australia, she once said, was her favorite. Her first trip was in 1934, when she won the women's bronc-riding event in the Melbourne Centennial show and entered the Sydney Royal Show. In 1939 she returned again, this time to defend her World Championship title in the Sidney Royal Show. She found the Australians a western ranch type people at heart—"rugged and easy to get along with."

Alice taught the actress Dale Evans, the wife of Roy Rogers, how to ride. She worked in pictures—made two in 1938, but according to her, "You have to sit around too much. There's too much waiting for shots." In addition to the Hollywood venture, the rider lassoed herself a bit of fame in journalism by writing magazine articles, one of which entitled, "What a Cowgirl Wants."

In 1942, the year after the saddle bronc event was closed

to women, Alice and a Tucson man called Joe Orr bought a rodeo of their own. They operated it for 14 years. In addition to producing the rodeo and handling the business end of its affairs, Alice rode broncs in every one of them they presented.

A reporter summed up Greenough's energetic routine in 1945: "Predawn rising, getting breakfast for the family and hired hands, cleaning up the ranchhouse, lending the boys outside a hand with branding or bronc busting, cooking a noon meal, then designing and making riding clothes, and in season, canning, preserving and salting down foods."

Before permanently relocating to Tucson in the 1970s, she started the Historical Museum in Red Lodge. She filled it with memorabilia from her own family. Even in retirement, Alice said that she "kept nine hours a day" at Wall's Livestock Supply and every chance she would get, she'd go down to her brother Frank's ranch at Sahuarita.

In 1975, Alice was the first person named to the Cowgirl Hall of Fame. In 1983, she was named to the Cowboy Hall of Fame. "The rodeo life was a good life," she said at the induction ceremony.

She died at her Tucson home in 1995 at age 93. The Greenough family maintained the ranch where she was born until the early 1990s.

Esther Combes Vance

(1903-1983)

The Life and Lure of Sidney Aviator

ONE DAY IN 1929, Esther Vance, a 26-year-old Montana pilot, received an invitation from another aviator—the greatly adored Amelia Earhart.

Earhart was already a celebrity of epic stature, a successful adventuress and author, a flashy brand and an on the ball business mind, a name and a face as recognizable as any in the country. A passionate advocate for the betterment of female pilots, Earhart had a new project circling in her mind—the formation of a nationwide club.

Vance, a Sidney High School graduate, was busily compiling her own set of credentials, too, performing aerial stunts with her husband while cutting her teeth as an independent pilot. Indeed, she distinguished herself one year earlier as the state of Montana's first licensed commercial woman pilot and the twenty-second woman in the United States to receive a limited commercial pilot's license.

Eligibility for membership in the group, wrote Earhart—who herself just one year earlier became the first woman passenger on a trans-Atlantic flight—would be extended to any woman holding a pilot's license issued by the Department of Commerce. Would Vance be interested in joining the first organization assembled of women aviators?

Perhaps answering yes was a no-brainer of sorts for Vance; when the group later issued its 99 charter memberships, one of them would be allotted to Vance. The goal of the club was to promote fellowship among licensed pilots and encourage more women to learn to fly. Earhart was elected its first president. The Ninety-Nines would even have their own official song.

Today, the presence of women pilots is no longer anomalous, and the group currently has thousands of members worldwide. And while she might not be a common name among first fliers, Esther Vance, in retrospect, was one of the earliest prototypes of the starry-eyed aviator.

Barnstorming in the Blood

ESTHER COMBES WAS BORN August 19, 1903, in Clinton, Indiana, the daughter of William and Dicy Pastre Combes. In 1906, the Combes family moved to Sidney, Montana, where William was enveloped in a variety of practices. He built furniture, served as a mortician, owned a movie theatre, and also fixed up apartment houses that he operated as rental properties. After viewing a young barnstormer's sideshow spectacle at a fair in Sidney, William added aviation to his expanding list of interests. After William experienced his first ride, he was so transfixed by the thrill of rising above the country and clouds that as soon as he touched down, he paid the same pilot to take up his two daughters, Esther, and her older sister, Geneva, next.

In the mid-1920s, William bought his first airplane, receiving flying lessons from a man named Earl Vance, a native of Indiana and a graduate of the Aberdeen Business School. Earl had arrived in Montana after completing flight training school in the army. Discharged in 1919 with the rank of second lieutenant, Earl's steered himself west.

In 1921 Esther graduated from Sidney High School and later the University of Washington in 1925, majoring in physical education and teaching. Returning to Sidney, she received a jam-packed introduction from her father to the art of flying; more than a hobby, William used his plane to transfer passengers at fairs and for his own businesses. And on top of this, Esther was charmed by his acquaintance and instructor, Earl Vance, about seven years her senior, who "sold her on the bright and glittering future of being an aviator's wife."

Esther and Earl were married in August 1925 and celebrated their honeymoon with a barnstorming tour to locations between Montana and Florida.

Lure of Flight Lessons and Love of Solo Adventures

AT FIRST ESTHER SERVED as business manager and treasurer of the commercial flying business that Earl started in Sidney called the Vance Air Service. "Time Flies Why Don't You?" was the company pitch. Esther, however, before long excelled in a new, exciting type of role at Vance Air Service; she would navigate the sky.

Esther enrolled in her first flight lesson in Florida when she and Earl were wintering there in 1926. Her 10 hours of instruction were spread over a period of two years. Though it sounds remarkably slim, she was able to make her solo flight after a mere 10 hours of instruction had been received. Ten hours of flight instruction was, according to one contemporary aviation magazine, "considered good for a woman student, although some women students have soloed with five- or six-hours' instruction, but the majority require 15 hours."

Esther later conceded that it would "have been better" had she received her instruction "regularly each day."

As it turned out, Esther and Earl relocated the base of the Vance Air Service's flight operations to Great Falls in 1927, where Esther oversaw the day-to-day requirements of the office, now on the airport north of the city. Still, she continued to challenge herself and to progress as a pilot.

Esther's first solo flight was made on March 3, 1928, from the Great Falls airport, during which she looped the field at an altitude of approximately 500 feet and then executed a successful landing. Her second flight was conducted that evening promptly after she had soloed.

On September 16, 1928, Esther Vance became licensed as a private pilot to fly all government licensed planes and subsequently as a limited commercial pilot to escort people on paid sight-seeing trips and make deliveries around the state. (To provide context, in the timeline of aviation, only one year earlier, Charles Lindbergh achieved world stature after he completed the first solo nonstop transatlantic flight in his plane, *The Spirit of St. Louis*.)

By 1930, in Montana, there were several female pilots who had received flight instruction and learned to fly, including Esther, Maurine Allen of Lewistown, and Anna Lou Schaeffer of Helena.

According to one contemporary newspaper account, "increasing interest is being shown in this field by women (in

Montana) in the last several
months, according to Mrs.
Vance and it is her belief
that within the next few
years women pilots will no
longer be unusual."

At five feet tall and
weighing between 90 and
95 pounds, Esther wasn't
the strongest or sturdiest of
pilots, but her size was by
no means an impediment
to her flying.

According to one story
about Esther published in
1930, "she has flown the Waco 9, three different Waco 10's,
the Monocoupe and had taken up the big four-passenger cabin
Stinson Detroiter and flown it for some distance although she
has not yet attempted to land this plane."

Although Esther described all of the planes as being very
simple to maneuver in the sky, she articulated a first-choice
fondness for the Monocoupe, a small light aircraft that, she
said, was the most natural match for her because of its compact-
ness: "Well, you see it's just my size. I crank it up and take it
out all by myself."

The article went on to emphasize the important role of
Esther's self-confidence in her aviation.

"Any fear or nervousness while in the air alone was denied
by Mrs. Vance, who stated that she particularly enjoyed pilot-
ing her own plane and gained much pleasure in flying in the
Waco open cock pit."

For a number of years, the Vances barnstormed their way

through the Midwest with Earl doing most of the flying and Esther on the ground promoting, the couple dropping in at rodeos or community events or other places that almost assuredly guaranteed a crowd. While this unusual type of business was unpredictable, Esther revealed herself to be a shrewd advertiser and spur-of-the-moment marketing whiz, informing a small town without little notice that the Vance airplane "was surveying an air route and to immediately wire back the location of their airport."

"This usually caused considerable confusion because most towns did not have an airport," said Vance. "We would then arrange for the community experts to pick an open field and meet with their (at that time non-existent) airport and aviation committee. The result was a red-carpet treatment with free meals, speeches and lots of publicity. We took time to haul all paying passengers available, with speeches by (Earl) in between."

Esther continued to serve as salesperson, business manager, and treasurer for the Vance Air Service until the business was destroyed by fire in 1931. Despite this unfortunate loss, Earl stayed active in aviation by working as a pilot for National Park Airways (a short-lived airline that operated in Montana in the 1920s and '30s) and later working as an aerial map maker for the United States Government. Esther's plane was destroyed in the fire, and she quit flying for a short period until her father came "to the aid of the Lady without a plane." William would give his daughter one of his own planes.

Realm of High Adventure

IN 1940 EARL VANCE returned to active service as a captain and training officer. During World War II he served as a base commander and ascended the ranks of major and colonel. He died prematurely at age 48 of a heart attack in 1944.

Esther appears to have abandoned flying altogether after her husband's death. Eventually, she removed to Missoula, where she worked in the registrar's office at the University of Montana until her retirement. She died May 25, 1983, aged 79.

While Esther Combes Vance was not as well-known and perhaps was not even as skilled as some of her counterparts, she was undoubtedly an astute, daring pilot who remained optimistic about the future arc and opportunity of women in aviation. She once succinctly explained her attitude, declaring:

"Women will no longer be able to resist the lure of flying. The air has ceased to be merely a substance in which we live and work and which we breathe. It has become a realm of high adventure; the air is ours to explore."

Dorothy Johnson

(1905-1984)

Western Epics, She Wrote

DOROTHY M. JOHNSON, a witty, gritty Western taleteller famous for such stories as "The Man Who Shot Liberty Valance," died Sunday, November 11, 1984, at her home in Missoula's West Rattlesnake Valley.

She was 78 and had suffered from Parkinson's disease and other illnesses for the final couple of years of her life. Before her death, the author of "The Hanging Tree," "The Bloody Bozeman," "A Man Called Horse," and many other short stories and magazine articles, specified that the inscription on her grave marker be "PAID."

"God and I know what it means," she said in an interview shortly before her death, "and nobody else needs to know."

Born Dec. 19, 1905, in McGregor, Iowa, to Lester E. and Louisa Barlow Johnson, Dorothy Marie Johnson moved to Great Falls, in 1909, and later Whitefish, in 1913. Johnson described her childhood in Whitefish in several lengthy magazine articles.

"The raw new town where I grew up—Whitefish, Montana—swarmed with money-hungry children who were willing to do almost anything to make an honest nickel. The trouble was that just about everything you could do was part of your normal chores, and you didn't get paid for it. Like filling the woodbox or lugging in a bucket of water while your mother admonished automatically, "Now don't hurt your back," or splitting kindling while she warned, "Now don't

chop your foot." Or feeding the chickens, carrying out the slop bucket, washing dishes, picking potato bugs and shoveling snow…After I explained gladly about allowances (it was seldom that I knew more about something than my parents did), they got the idea across tactfully that maybe some children in some places received allowances but no such outlandish custom was going to be introduced in Whitefish, anyway not at our house. That was back in the days when parents and children could still communicate with no trouble."

Johnson published several articles about her childhood in *Montana The Magazine of Western History*. Her nonfiction conveys her love of Montana and her interpretation of the West's uniqueness. She described Whitefish as a "raw new town," filled with opportunity credited to the jobs created by the Great Northern Railroad. For the workers attracted to Whitefish, it was "the anteroom of paradise . . . the promised land, flowing with milk and honey. All they had to do to enjoy it was work."

In one of her writings, the diligent, reliable men and women of Whitefish stood out against the "rich people and Eastern dudes" she encountered in Glacier National Park. When she wrote of the social divide she noticed among visitors to the park, she viewed it in terms of an East-West split: "We unrich Westerners were suspicious of the whole lot of them. We looked down on them because we thought they looked down on us. But they didn't even see us, which made the situation even more irritating. Years later, when I lived in a big Eastern city, I learned not to see strangers. . . . But in the uncrowded West, in my country, it's bad manners, and on the trail it's proper to acknowledge the existence of other human beings and say hello."

Reared a widow's daughter, she graduated from White-fish High School in 1922 and studied premed at Montana State College in Bozeman before transferring to Montana State University in Missoula. By the time she graduated with a B A. degree in English in 1928, she had already published her first poem. She was married briefly with the last name of Peterkin.

After graduation, she found work as a stenographer in an Okanogan, Washington, department store. After another stenographer position in Menasha, Wisconsin, she spent fifteen years as a magazine editor in New York City at Gregg Publishing Company and Farrell Publishing Corporation.

From 1944-50 Johnson also edited a women's magazine in New York City; she eventually returned to Whitefish where she became news editor of the *Whitefish Pilot* (1950-1953).

In 1953, she returned to the University of Montana as a member of the journalism faculty. She once told students, "One of the perils of going to the university is that you are liable to hear me tell you how to get on a horse three or four times before you graduate. Writers are like students—they sometimes have to learn things they don't even want to know. Getting on a horse was part of the necessary information I had to learn."

Harold Guy (H. G.) Merriam, professor emeritus of English at the University of Montana and an American Rhodes scholar, and a major influence in Johnson's early writing development, later said of her:

"She wrote prodigiously—story after story. I felt from the beginning that she had a real talent for them I think the reason for her success was that she kept right at it; she didn't letup...."

Johnson wrote sixteen books, beginning with "Beulah Bunny Tells All" in 1941 and ending with "All the Buffalo Returning" in 1979. Johnson's most popular work, "The Man Who Shot Liberty Valence," is simultaneously a period piece and an eternal tale of payback, love and honor redeemed that climaxes in a shootout. Johnson's prose is graceful, and while her short stories might be standard, they're also always transfixing and nuanced, with subtle forms of irony at each turn. Eventually turned into a western movie classic (1962) directed by John Ford, starring John Wayne and James Stewart, this is one of Johnson's short stories that has endured.

In 1959, *The Hanging Tree* also became an unforgettable western movie. Gary Cooper, a fellow Montanan, starred in *The Hanging Tree*, and once gave Miss Johnson a pheasant wishbone which she copper plated and wore as a necklace.

Ultimately, Johnson was a complete and ideal Westerner, and this helped her do extremely well in a literary genre that tended to be dominated with male bylines. Johnson affirmed women's ability to write Westerns: "After all, men who write about the Frontier West weren't there either. We all get our historical background material from the same printed sources. An inclination to write about the frontier is not a sex-linked characteristic, like hair on the chest."

Though Johnson never self-identified as a trailblazer or an activist, she was, according to one friend, a "witty, gritty little bobcat of a woman," and her writings reflect her western strength of mind. Irascible and curmudgeon, Johnson shunned pretension, both in her writing and her personal life. An example of this took place in Missoula in 1979 at a conference entitled "Who Owns the West?" when Johnson delivered her assigned lecture called "the Revisionist Western Novel."

"The revisionist western novel is the one where the young girl hitchhikes on a wagon train from Boston to Fort Bullfrog, where she begins a day-care center, a food co-op, and starts a consciousness-raising group."

"All sorts of vexed-looking young women were staring gape-mouthed at Dorothy," noted one of the attendees.

Following her death, a memorial service was held in Missoula on Wednesday, November 14, 1984. Her body was cremated, and the ashes interred in Whitefish Cemetery next to the grave of her mother.

L. RON HUBBARD

(1911-1986)

How the Seeds of Scientology Were Shaped in the Flathead Valley and Western Montana

WHEN L. RON HUBBARD, the founder of the Church of Scientology, died on January 24, 1986, mystery encircled his death just as it had cloaked the final decades of his life.

Hubbard started Scientology in the early 1950s as a program of spiritual ideas called Dianetics. The advent of the Dianetics theory appeared in *The Explorers Journal*, with members and associates of the Explorers Club the first to examine his official description of it. Hubbard's religiosity and grand exploration were both byproducts of traveling to so many far-flung lands through a greater quest for answers to be developed in Scientology, which was significantly influenced by a number of decisive years spent in western Montana.

Hubbard was born on March 13, 1911, in Tilden, Nebraska. After moving from his birthplace, he spent his first two years in Durant, Oklahoma, where his grandfather Lafayette Waterbury had established a horse ranch. His grandfather, known as Lafe, was described as "a big buff man, hail fellow well met, friend to all the world," according to the Hubbard biography *Bare-Faced Messiah*. Lafe and his wife produced a son and six daughters, including Hubbard's mother Ledora May. His father, Harry Ross Hubbard, served in the United States Navy during Hubbard's early years.

When his father returned from service, the Hubbard-Waterbury family moved to Kalispell, where Hubbard's grandfa-

ther acquired several dozen
acres of land for the breed-
ing of blooded mustangs
and owned several "famous
studs." His father worked
at a local newspaper. It
was also in Kalispell that
Hubbard said, at just 3 and
half years old, he learned
to read, write and ride a
range bronco named Nancy
Hanks, he recalled in the
biography *Master Mariner:
At the Helm Across Seven
Seas,* "with a single snaffle bit, no quirt, no spurs and a cut
down McClellan cavalry saddle, the skirts of which had to be
amputated so as to get the doghouse stirrups high enough for
me to reach them." He claimed that he had photos to prove
that he was writing well at such a young age. The story that
Hubbard retold was one of "an early bond of friendship"
formed in the fall of 1914 as the young man danced to the
beat of Indian drums and impressed Blackfeet Indians at a
tribal ceremony held on the outskirts of town. (Several critics
later writing exposes of Scientology dismissed his tale as fanci-
ful and "pure fiction.")

"I lived in the typical West with its do-and-dare attitudes,
its wry humor, cowboy pranks and make nothing of the worst
and most dangerous," he said in *Master Mariner.* "The weather
of Montana is of course brutal. The country is immense and
swallows men up rather easily hence they have to live bigger
than life to survive. There were still Indians around living in
forlorn and isolated tepees, the defeated race, making beauti-

fully threaded buckskin gauntlets and other foofaraw. Notable amongst them was an Indian called "Old Tom" who was sufficiently dirty and outlaw and interesting, a full-fledged Blackfoot medicine man, to be a small boy's dream."

Hubbard moved one year later with his family to "The Old Homestead" outside of Helena. In some of his biographical notes, he wrote, "I grew up with old frontiersmen, cowboys, and had an Indian medicine man as one of my best friends. Until I was 10, I lived the hard life of the West ... in a land of 40-degree-below blizzards and vast spaces." He later spoke of his first real home, "Old Brick," a property that stood at the corner of Fifth Avenue and Beattie Street in Helena. It served as the home for the entire Hubbard-Waterbury family, including grandparents, Hubbard and his six sisters, Harry Ross, Ledora and a feisty bull terrier named Liberty Bill.

He became a world traveler at the age of 10, thanks to his father's Navy career, and began his writing discipline by keeping a diary of his travels. After Ross was promoted to lieutenant in the Navy in 1921, the Hubbards embarked on a life of constant movement, relocating almost yearly to posts in Guam, San Diego, Seattle and Bremerton in the state of Washington, and Washington, D.C.

Hubbard always returned to Helena in those early years and attended Helena High School in 1927-28, where he wrote for the school newspaper. He regarded Helena fondly as his "hometown," according to his early journals, and recounted some of his adventures in a piece in the *Helena Daily Independent* in 1927. One of the highlights of his travels was witnessing an execution in China, according to the article. He also noted that he had the "distinction of being the only boy in the country to secure an Eagle Scout badge at the age of 12 years," which he did while in Washington, D.C. The 1928

Helena High School yearbook has a photo of the staff of the bi-monthly school paper, *The Nugget*, including thickly red-haired Ronald Hubbard, one of two "joke editors." His friends called him "Brick."

Years later, Hubbard dropped out of George Washington University in 1932 and tried his luck at freelance journalism but soon quit in favor of pulp fiction writing. Most pulp fiction writers told exaggerated tales: mass-market, action-packed stories published in cheaply produced magazines. Dianetics was pitched and written as science fiction, but by the summer of 1950, Dianetics was making its advance up the best-seller lists, and by August 1950, more than 500 "Dianetics clubs" had sprung up across the nation. "A new cult is smoldering across the U.S. underbrush," declared *Time* magazine on July 24, 1950.

The wandering spirit of Hubbard's childhood in Montana stimulated a lifelong love for adventure, and according to Vaughan Young, author of a Hubbard biography, Hubbard attributed his success partly to the "rough and tough atmosphere" of Kalispell and Helena ranch life. He was a dreamer who saw himself as the hero of his own rich adventure story. Considerably less kinder assessments of Hubbard can be located in a number of court records, affidavits and even some of Hubbard's own early writings, which present the founder of Scientology as a natural-born fabulist whose claims contained many embellishments, joined with, in many instances, out-and-out fabrications.

Hubbard later renamed Dianetics as Scientology, which took hold as a basis of religious beliefs and practices. Two researchers sent on behalf of the Church of Scientology, Pam Schwartz and Mary Pirak, of Hollywood, California, even visited Helena in January 1975 to research Hubbard's roots

and promote their church. There was no Church of Scientology in Montana, they said; the closest were in Salt Lake City
and Omaha. (To this day, no Scientology church has found
root in Montana.) Scientology remains a prevalent religion in
Hollywood circles today.

Hubbard last visited Montana in 1975 when he and his
father came for the funeral of his maternal grandfather. His
mother died in 1959. His parents and maternal grandparents
are buried in Forestvale Cemetery near Helena. In a profile
of Hubbard in *The New York Times* around that time, the
author's behavior was described as increasingly erratic. While
his fortunes had swelled, his friendships had dwindled, almost
to the point of his full isolation. He resigned his leadership
position in the church in 1966 to devote himself to writing.
But he hadn't been heard from, and even church representatives usually had difficulty pinpointing his whereabouts. A
lawsuit by his son to have him declared dead or incompetent
was thrown out in July 1975 by a California judge. Hubbard
refused to appear at any of the proceedings, and he spent his
later years outside the public eye.

Yet, in 1984, two years before his death at age 74, the reclu-
sive science fiction writer opened up one final time to a biographer and recalled how he spent "the most memorable parts
of his youth" at Kalispell and "The Old Homestead" outside
Helena. He recalled that he never was allowed to ride any of the
blooded stock bred by his grandfather, only range broncs and
mustangs. "It did not matter how often I was thrown," he said.
"When a mustang exploded under me, goaded on by a frozen
saddle blanket, it was I who was always scolded and cautioned
not to be mean to the horses. It never seemed to surprise these
adults that I remained alive under all this."

Maurice Hilleman

(1911-2005)

Eastern Montana Farm Boy Who Changed—and Saved—the World

MAURICE HILLEMAN'S MOTHER DIED from eclampsia two days after he was delivered and his twin sister stillborn. Born in Miles City during the most wretched influenza pandemic in history—the Spanish Flu—and at a time when childhood diseases took the lives of thousands, Maurice somehow escaped death.

Forever influenced by this trauma, he made it his life's labor to see that others could do the same: receive another chance to live. The eventual inventor of approximately 40 vaccines, including many of the most common now administered, Hilleman's determination saved untold millions from disease.

Farming Upbringing; Tended Chickens

MAURICE HILLEMAN came from a farming upbringing that would serve as ideal preparation for a scientist to concoct life-rescuing vaccines. Born Saturday morning, August 30, 1919, Hilleman was the youngest of eight children of Anna and Gustave Hillemann (strong anti-German sentiment following the conclusion of World War I forced his parents to drop the second "n" on Maurice's birth certificate). Of no-nonsense parentage, his great-uncle had served as an Indian scout in the United States cavalry in the days following Custer's murder at the Battle of the Greasy Grass. Maurice and his siblings were named after resilient characters in the Elsie Dinsmore books,

a children's book series written between 1867 and 1905 about a devout orphan Christian girl.

Before she died of brain swelling caused from complications of childbirth, Anna asked Gustave to take care of the seven older children but to send Maurice to be raised by his aunt and uncle, a childless couple, named Robert and Edith. Since Maurice lived within a hundred yards of his biological father and siblings, he grew up on the family farm, the Riverview Garden and Nursery, outside Miles City, where he performed many tasks: picking beans and berries, weeding patches, bringing in the horses, and selling anything that people would purchase: tomatoes, potatoes, lettuce, radishes, cabbage, squash, corn, cottage cheese, and pumpkins.

The family sold brooms made from the straw of sorghum sugar and performed a number of landscaping services, from tree rehabilitation and removal, to spraying the trees to reduce worms and insect manifestations. They raised perennials and annuals and sold flowers, usually on Sundays, to the local florist.

"At one time (our farm) provided an escape for thieves and outlaws who were (being) pursued by vigilante posses from Miles City," Hilleman recalled in the early 2000s. "There was still a tall cottonwood on the high ground that carried a hangman's noose in its branches…When I was old enough to tell the difference between a weed and a plant, I was sent out into the sun, working from sunup to sunset."

On the family farm, Maurice learned agronomy, electrical work, blacksmithing and tool construction. He dismantled irrigation pumps and then rebuilt them to better understand mechanics. For the sake of knowledge, he restored a wrecked 1928 Ford into a functioning motor vehicle. "When you're brought up on a farm, you have a lot of general knowledge," he once said.

Maurice also tended to chickens, keeping the coop clean, feeding and watering, and collecting eggs to bring to market, a life experience that would come in beneficial years later.

Early in his life, Hilleman learned that in Montana you were responsible for yourself and that nobody was out looking for you. When he was eight years old, he almost died of suffocation by diphtheria and was declared dead. One time, he nearly was flattened by a freight train on a narrow bridge hustling over the Tongue River. On another occasion, at the height of flood time, he and his brother bought a small flatbed boat from a hobo for one dollar and rowed the rickety thing down the Yellowstone. Though the family farm was situated on the banks of the Tongue and Yellowstone rivers, Maurice couldn't swim. He barely made it back to the edge of the river, covered in mud. He ran back home in a panic and told his aunt Edith how he had nearly drowned. She barely raised an eyebrow and said nothing while continuing to silently wash the family's clothes. "She was Lutheran," Hilleman recalled. "She figured that when your time had come, your time had come."

His biological father was a devout Lutheran, a domineering man who had expected that Maurice and his brothers would become ministers of the faith. (In one of the strangest incongruities of medicine, Maurice was not allowed to have any vaccines.) But his uncle Robert was an iconoclastic and free-thinking life insurance salesman who encouraged Maurice

to question the conventional wisdom and philosophy of his
parents. Robert's influence rubbed off early on Maurice. One
Sunday morning, the minister of the Missouri Synod Lutheran
Church in Custer County caught young Maurice reading
Charles Darwin's *The Origin of Species* during the service. The
minister attempted to confiscate Darwin's tract on evolution
from the child. "I told the minister that the book belonged to
the public library, and I was going to turn him in if he took it
from me," Hilleman later recalled. "I was enthralled by Darwin
because the church was so opposed to him."

His first hero was Howard Taylor Ricketts, a pathologist
from the Midwest who worked in the Bitterroot Valley of
Montana and at the University of Chicago on Rocky Mountain spotted fever.

"A Basement Boy" at J.C. Penney

At Custer County High School Hilleman had the choice
of majoring in academics, business, general farming, or science.
He picked the latter. All of his brothers made the same decision
and were similarly successful.

Following his graduation in 1937, Maurice went to work
as assistant manager at the local J.C. Penney store, starting as
"a basement boy"—a respectable, stable position in Eastern
Montana in the bitter clutch of the Great Depression—helping "cowpokes pick out chenille bathrobes for their girlfriends."
One of his brothers prodded their father to send Maurice to
college; he acquiesced.

"If you lived in Miles City and you were smart," Hilleman
once said, "you went to Concordia College and then to the
seminary to be ordained as a Lutheran preacher. But I wasn't
going to do that."

Too underprivileged to afford the $45-a-term tuition, Maurice applied for and won a full scholarship from Montana State University, and after graduating from MSU with majors in microbiology and chemistry in 1941, Hilleman won a fellowship to the University of Chicago. After Hilleman earned his Ph.D. in microbiology and chemistry, he made vaccine research and development the central purpose of his career. "He was motivated by one thing—he wanted to try and make vaccines for every disease that could possibly hurt or kill a child," said friend, colleague and biographer Paul A. Offit, MD.

A Montanan Who Got Things Done

FROM THE ONSET OF HIS CAREER, Maurice Hilleman attributed his interest in biology to growing up resourcefully on an isolated farm, and he credited some of his capacity to "get things done"—i.e., weakening viruses in laboratory cells and eliminating diseases in the US through vaccines—to lessons that educated him as a child.

"In Montana, things get done," said Hilleman. "You put up a barn, a fence, a gate. These were project events. Then everybody would go out, get a fresh bucket of water, sit on a log and pass around a cup to celebrate. It's the same feeling you have when you get a vaccine licensed."

In 1944, he received his Doctor of Philosophy degree from the University of Chicago, and one year later was awarded the Howard Taylor Ricketts award (named after his first hero) by that university. He was commended in 1955 for discovering an entirely new family of viruses which cause respiratory disease, such as virus pneumonia and acute sore throat, named by Hilleman as the "RI Viruses."

In early April 1957, he read a news bulletin about thousands of mothers in Hong Kong and their long lines of sick, glossy-eyed children and predicted that the next flu pandemic had arrived. He authored and issued a press release on May 22, 1957 predicting to the world that there would be a nasty pandemic when school started in the fall.

Preemptively, Hilleman injected the virus specimen from a Navy soldier into chicken eggs to produce a vaccine and sent virus samples to manufacturers; approximately forty million doses of vaccine were quickly produced in the United States to inoculate against the Asian Flu, perhaps saving tens of thousands of lives. (About 116,000 Americans died from the Asian Flu pandemic).

While researching a vaccine for measles, Hilleman discovered that many chicken eggs were contaminated with a highly contagious bird virus, so he went in search of chickens producing virus-free eggs. He found them at Kimber Farms in California, except the farm was quite reluctant to provide its birds to science. That was, until the Montana expatriate running the farm, Helena native W.F. Lamoreux, found out that Hilleman also was a Montanan. After learning of the shared connection, Lamoreux allowed Hilleman to "take them all" at the generous price of "one buck apiece." Consequently, the first measles vaccine was established through the participation of a flock of chickens and a virologist and a chicken breeder both born and raised in Montana.

"Montana blood runs very thick," Hilleman once recounted. "And chicken blood runs even thicker with me."

Mumps Vaccine Created From Daughter's Sickness

ONE OF HIS MORE significant achievements was the development of the mumps vaccine in 1963, when his five-year-old daughter,

Jeryl Lynn, was afflicted with a case of the disease, which infected approximately a million people in the United States every year. Named the JLH strain, it was made from the virus that infected his daughter. (At the time of his daughter's infection, Hilleman was widowed. Only a few months earlier, Thelma, a fellow Custer County High School graduate, who married Maurice in Miles City on New Year's Eve, 1944, died of breast cancer.)

"As with his work on influenza virus, Hilleman turned to chickens," wrote Paul A. Offit. MD. "When he got back to the laboratory, he took the broth containing Jeryl's virus and inoculated it into an incubating hen's egg; in the center of the egg was an unborn chick. During the next few days, the virus grew in the membrane that surrounded the chick embryo."

The mumps vaccine was licensed in 1967. Hilleman and his team then developed techniques for cultivating and reducing the effect of the virus in duck eggs, opening the way to a rubella vaccine, which was licensed and distributed in 1969. Around that time Hilleman decided to combine his measles, mumps, and rubella into a single shot, later known as MMR.

One of his Hilleman's most important innovations was the first vaccine effective against hepatitis B, approved in 1981. He was also the first to develop and mass-market the pneumococcal and chickenpox vaccines.

Toward the end of his life, the damning charge was leveled against him by a British physician that MMR caused autism. Although multiple independent studies showed that MMR never caused autism and the physician was later charged with misconduct for not revealing his unethical financial ties with seedy personal injury lawyers, the allegations caused an international stir.

Influence of Hilleman Infinite

A WELL-RESPECTED TITAN in scientific circles, he might be, according to one colleague quoted in Forbes at the time of his death, "the single most influential public health figure of the twentieth century because of his vaccine research and development." All the while, however, he remains something of an unrecognized genius, in no small part because "he was not someone disposed to taking personal credit for his achievements," said Anthony S. Fauci, the director of the National Institute of Allergy and Infectious Diseases (and later the highly contentious COVID czar), to a symposium on Hilleman in 2005.

"He was always quick to give credit to his team members," said Fauci. "It was never about him...despite Maurice's enormous accomplishments, his name has never been a household word."

"Here was a guy," said Walter Strauss, senior director of epidemiology research at Merck, to author Paul A. Offit, MD., "born on some windswept ranch in Montana, practically orphaned at birth, taken in by relatives, and who, but for his talent and drive, might have spent a lifetime working as a clerk at a retail store. Instead, he rose to the pinnacle of scientific achievement in the United States, leaving his mark on half the world's children. It is one of the greatest of all Horatio Alger stories."

Maurice Ralph Hilleman died April 11, 2005, at age 85, perhaps the most important person ever born and raised in Montana.

BILL STOCKTON

(1921-2002)

'Crazy' Sheepherder-Artist Who Worked
Beyond 'the Pulling Taste'

"PEOPLE THINK I AM CRAZY," said Bill Stockton on the subject
of the most common judgment of him. A sign painter and
commercial artist- illustrator who developed creative standards
that would be "beyond the pulling taste," Stockton always
stayed true to his greatest and considered by some craziest
personal loves: ranching and abstract art.

Son of Fergus County homesteaders, Bill was born in 1921
and raised in Winnett and Grass Range; the Grass Range
High School graduate left Central Montana to join the armed
forces and later become a commercial artist, studying at the
Minneapolis School of Art and then at the Ecole de la Grande
Chaumiere in Paris.

At a time when he was reaping the fulfillment of a viable
career, he said that he had "a change of heart," and he and his
wife (whom he met in France) removed to a ranch a few miles
west of Grass Range.

In the midst of the wrinkled hills of the Grass Range country, Stockton built "a modern home," a structure that was
"itself a work of modern art," according to one account. He
spent most of his summer months ranching to support himself
and his family of four while the winter was reserved for his
other profession as an artist. "That's why you see so much white
in my paintings," he told a newspaper in July 1958.

From the stony, edgy silence of the plains, he dedicated

himself to the avant-garde
movement of painting, an
abstract expressionism born
out of eminent Pablo Picasso's Cubism.

He restricted his skill to
a tiny space, a small room
so filled to capacity with
paints, easels and drawings
and sketches that it was once
written that no two persons
could comfortably coexist in
the studio at the same time.

He once said that his goal as an artist was "to organize
nature" and transcribe it into "the abstract, into pure geometri-
cal form." Deviating from Picasso's Cubism, which was enam-
ored of the creation and use of a third-dimension illusion,
Stockton ignored that dimension and transferred its multi-
faceted designs into only two dimensions. A typical Montana
scene painted by Stockton would have sacrificed details and
nuances for an emphasis on typical marks of the isolated country. He had "no heart or desire," said Stockton, to produce
the conventionally familiar type of painting which the average
viewer would understand, which he called "potboilers," though
he sometimes grudgingly produced them to produce sales.
However, his passion wasn't in the familiar, or in the genera-
tion of art that most people instinctively would call pretty and
clamor to hang in their living rooms. Such paintings would've
been too exacting, too imitative. If the viewer wanted the
precise copying of nature, they would be better off purchasing
a cheap copy of a photograph. Indeed, Stockton excelled in the
abstract blending of supreme colors and harmonious forms.

"Most people think of an artist as a craftsman who can imitate something to their taste...But this is not the purpose of an artist...an artist takes the ordinary and makes something interesting out of it...He can't cling to the subject. Nature is disorganized order...It is the task of the painter to organize it just like the musician organizes noise to compose a melody and the writer organizes disorganized life to create literature."

What looked insignificant to the average eye could fascinate him. It could be a painting of a rock formation or a number of other subjects that he could find anywhere without seeking. Perhaps it could be a pattern of boulder slabs or a curiously triangle of trees that thrilled him, and he would not rest until he had relocated it with his paints.

One of Stockton's more popular paintings, "Bus Stop," however, didn't necessarily represent his abstract school of painting. Stockton claimed that he didn't know the name of the subject—a stranger. He said that he had seen her in "a small bus stop restaurant" and that concise impression had inspired him to paint the features as he remembered them.

He told one art publication in 1958 that he hoped for recognition beyond "the relatively small groups of experts" who admired his art, but he believed that his chances were slight.

"A recent poll in New York revealed that of 100 fine artists, only seven or eight were able to make a living with their work," Stockton said. "Fifty of the artists had a monthly income of less than $200."

Still, Stockton believed enough in the power of art that he taught it both in colleges and privately.

"Both his philosophy and his livelihood are those of a man of the soil," John Armstrong, Director of the Yellowstone Art Center in Billings, said in 1973. "His art has a moral honesty that seems difficult to find in much art today."

Stockton's quirky juggling of occupations and unique skill set reinforced the view that he was a man of distinction. Medium-hopping at his leisure, his art spanned a range from abstract-expressionist paintings and metal sculptures to light fixtures and furniture.

There was no shortage of acknowledgment among artists and art lovers for Stockton's work. Many ranchers felt a responsive nerve when they viewed Stockton's sheep renditions; one exhibit of his sheep paintings was described by an art guide "as explicit and down-to-earth as the woolgrower-artist who created them."

His paintings were accepted for entry in various national exhibitions, and he was represented in, according to one estimate, about 200 private collections in New York, Tulsa, Billings, Bozeman, San Francisco and even in France.

One Montana newspaper editor heralded Stockton as "perhaps the finest artist Montana has produced since Charlie Russell," and portrayed the shrewd individualist equally as committed to sheep ranching, which, he proudly on one occasion pointed out, produced food and clothing for people.

"I really have more respect for a good sheepherder than an artist," said Stockton in 1973. "The sheepherder functions in society. I produce food and clothing for 90 people here."

He died at his Grass Range home in 2002.

Orville "Cowboy" Carlson

(1923-1996)

Ekalaka Cowpuncher Turned Show-Biz Wrestler

HE WAS A BONA FIDE RANCHER before he established himself in the center of the high-flying, excitable, carnival-tinged wrestling world; the stage nickname "Cowboy" was a natural extension of his identity.

In short time, Orville Lee Carlson became a mainstay in the grapple and grunt-and-groan game's golden age, meeting the most hyped villains in the Northwest, West and Southwest states.

Born in Milwaukee, Wisconsin, September 28, 1923 (his military draft record lists 1923; his death certificate states 1922), to Oscar Carlson and Mabel Wilberg, Orville was raised in eastern Montana, in the Ekalaka area, and started amateur wrestling when he was 14 years old and won two state titles by the time he was 17.

He started breaking horses when he was 14 and found strenuous work riding rough critters in and around the Powder River country. This trade made Carlson a natural for competitive rodeo riding. While he was at some of the rodeos, he often picked up extra cash by accepting the challenge of the men in the athletic shows who offered to best anyone within a certain time limit in grappling contests.

While he was in the U.S. Army at Camp Lee and Camp Pickett, Virginia, he won the Golden Gloves title as well as gaining a duo of wrestling championships.

After the war Carlson went back to rodeo work and in October 1947, he broke his shoulder participating in a rodeo in stadium in Chicago; the fall from the horse ending his competition in that show. Another interesting event of his trip was that he had the room in the Royalton Hotel next to "Okaganan Paul of Montana," who fatally stabbed a man during a dispute erupting from a game card. When Orville came up to his room, he was greeted by the chaotic aftermath, which included a stretcher transporting one of the survivors of the stabbing wrath of "the Montana Indian."

Carlson entered the bizarre world of scripted wrestling by accident. After the spending the bulk of savings to travel from Montana to the Houston Fat Stock Show and Livestock Exhibition to compete in a rodeo there, the Cowboy needed some extra loot to eat on, so he went to the wrestling matches in Houston and challenged any man in the arena. He later said that he turned to the mat when he suffered a broken shoulder in a rodeo spill and decided it "just wasn't worth it." Whether he was referring to the earlier tumble in Chicago and whether he suffered an additional bad injury in Houston is unclear.

Promoter Morris Siegel, a New York transplant who had found a niche at promoting boxing and wrestling cards, agreed to give him a chance on the next week's card. Siegel put on regular Friday-night cards at the City Auditorium in downtown Houston for more than forty years. The massive brown stone palace held four thousand.

About 25-years old at the time, Carlson's blonde hair, blue eyes, and light complexion must have impressed Siegel, who knew that the real competition in his game was the one for attention. Indeed, the promoter saw something marketable: the ideal American male who was stoic, quiet, and dignified. The rugged northerner's good looks and appealing mien made him a "babyface," the wrestling term for the grappler who plays the good guy in the ring, as opposed to the villain, or "heel." After the Second World War, America was reforming and the television came and took hold and professional wrestling became hugely popular, an improbably successful industry, and Carlson became a fixture of the faux, lowbrow sport. Cowboy's first match in Houston found him without equipment or much wardrobe so he wrestled barefooted and in blue jeans.

The Cowboy enjoyed the staged experience of the mat so well that he quickly decided to make entertainment wrestling his profession and to use the rodeo as his hobby. He liked the humble Cowboy shtick and so did the fans, so he added cowboy type wrestling shoes to accompany the blue jeans and a Western hat when he entered or left the ring.

His favorite hold was a bull-dog headlock, which he called his "Powder River Hoolahan Hold," driving his opponent's face into the mat and then applying a half nelson and body press to pin his hapless foe.

His appearance and ability got him noticed and he soon gained entrée to the small-time Houston promoters. They offered him work wrestling opening matches in small towns within driving distance of the city. Cowboy formed connections with the right people, including Dory Funk, the progenitor of the first family of Texas wrestling, who frequently appeared in tag team and triple tag team matches with him. Cowboy was a popular draw in the Lone Star State for many years—and Dory must have factored heavily in this influence.

"I grew up on the Flying Mare Ranch, southwest of Amarillo, Texas," said Dory Funk Jr. "My brother Terry and I were standing in the shadow of a very famous man (Dory Funk Sr.,). It was not until I was finishing up college that I made the decision that I wanted to become a professional wrestler. Even though my hero was my father, training in the ring was by people he had a hand in training. Ricky Romero was my head coach. However, I received training from Bob Geigel, Verne Gagne, Joe Scarpello, Eddie Graham, Cowboy Carlson, Pedro Morales, and more on the wrestling mat in our garage, or in the ring."

All of these names listed by Funk are familiar ones in the history of show-business wrestling; for example, Gagne was the owner and promoter of the Minneapolis-based American Wrestling Association, the biggest promotion throughout the Midwest and Manitoba for many years. Yet Carlson's appreciation is unsung.

Nonetheless, he was no lower echelon performer and seems to have received a "push" on the Western wrestling circuit; controlling the results enabled promoters to give certain wrestlers a "push," building career momentum and an audience by ensuring a string of victories. He routinely appeared in newspaper ads promoting events throughout the region, especially the Tucson/Phoenix and Bellingham/Seattle areas.

One newspaper from 1951 said that the "handsome cowpuncher" was undefeated in the Bellingham, Washington area where he had become "the favorite of local fans."

Many of the fans who attended such events believed that the action was real, and promoters fanned the most lustful elements of their desires with the lure and promise of great violence. One billboard promoting a main event six-man tag team match, two out of three falls, pitting Cowboy Carlson, Andre Drapp and Paul Boesch versus Duke Keomuka, Great Yamato and Leo Newman, was advertised as a "legal riot": "Riots haven't been legalized in Texas, but there'll be one Monday night at the North Side Coliseum with plenty of policemen handy to protect the customers."

When the promoters told the wrestlers who the winners

were to be each night, each pair of combatants would put their heads together in the locker room to choreograph. Once the ending and a few maneuvers were agreed upon, much of what happened in the ring was improvised. In 1955, Carlson defeated Gorgeous George at the Tucson Sports Center before a packed house of 3,500 screaming fans. Known for his dyed goldilocks and outrageous strut and pompous bluster, Gorgeous George (1915-1963) was one of the most popular wrestlers of the sport's first golden age in the 1940s-1950s. Gorgeous George was known for his flamboyantly outrageous ring attire—pink robes, bejeweled dog collar, the finest fabrics, ruffles and lace—as well as his platinum bleached hair and myriad of indestructibly well-manicured curls and waves. The burly prima donna took a sound beating from Cowboy in losing the main event. In the best of three contests, Carlson won the first and third falls.

Cowboy traveled continuously and wrestled in most all large cities in the United States. Throughout the 1950s, Carlson spent time in Broadus in between circuit touring, "exercising, fishing with his family and relaxing."

He was often accompanied on tour with his wife, Ramona Kromlich. On October 25, 1942, Carlson married Ramona in Broadus. They had two children, a girl named Mona and a boy named David. It seems as if, at the peak of his busiest scheduling, the lengthiest time that he stayed in Montana when he wasn't booked in the arenas was about a month. One stretch lasted 18 months without a return trip home. An article in the 1955 *Billings Gazette* said that "Mrs. Carlson went on the circuit with her husband until her two children became school age. Since that time, she has made her home permanently in Broadus where she and her husband grew up and attended local schools."

Carlson was said to have made various retirements and comebacks, and, according to one wrestling database, wrestled matches all the way into the early 1970s. Modern records attempting to piece together the number of matches and event locations for period wrestlers such as Cowboy Carlson are notoriously incomplete. It doesn't seem as if Cowboy was ever turned in to the "heel," or bad guy.

Some guys made real money at it, however, the majority wrestled for little or average pay. In 1948, one high-earning "babyface" made $28,000 a year working all the time, wrestling fifty-one weeks a year, almost ten times Mr. and Mrs. Smith's annual household income. "Cowboy" was probably a middle-of-the-road earner.

For many years, the Carlson family careened around the country in a secondhand sedan, as excited as they were flat broke. Other times, Cowboy and a carload of other wrestlers would risk life and limb to get to the next booking only to find that bad weather had caused the matches to be canceled. At times, Cowboy sustained nasty injuries that sidelined him. Even with a script, punches slipped and heads collided, and that kind of mistake meant a broken nose, or cracked vertebrae, or slackened teeth. Cracked ribs were so common they were even discussed.

For at least 20 years, he took the bumps and the pain, accepting them as facts of wrestling life and the means to his personal ends. Then one day he packed away the ring trunks and said goodbye to the gimmicks and struts and all of the showbiz stuff and returned to the ranching life in eastern Montana.

On November 17, 1956, Custer County issued a divorce decree in Ramona's favor citing the grounds of "extreme cruelty." In October 1966, Carlson, 43, married Susan Yellow-eyes, 24, of Billings. Susie, an eye-ravishing Northern Cheyenne, was born in Ashland, Montana, on March 11, 1942 and died in Billings, December 11, 2006. Orville Lee "Cowboy" Carlson died after suffering cardiopulmonary arrest while at his home in Ashland, July 11, 1996.

THE TERRY MONTANA COWBOY BAND VISIT PRESIDENT COOLIDGE

IN 1927

TERRY AND PRAIRIE COUNTY stake claim to one piece of Montana's most idiosyncratic history—a band of musicians who invited themselves to a president's birthday party, and made his friendship in the process.

First called Joubert's Landing in recognition of the man who built the supply route along the Yellowstone River, Terry was renamed after Alfred Howe Terry, a general in the Union Army who commanded forces in the Dakota Territory after the Civil War. The original Terry Cornbelt Band formed in Terry, in 1909, one year before Terry was incorporated.

At that time, Terry would have been a double railroad town, influenced by the presence of the Northern Pacific and Milwaukee Railroads. Most of the original members were business men from Terry, but some were considered genuine "cowboys" while others hailed from other nearby towns, including Fallon, where the bandleader, Carl Anderson, lived. Their purpose was simple: a group of musicians who looked to supply their communities with good quality music and the promise of a jolly time.

After splitting, the group reemerged in 1915 with a fundraising dance held to secure funds for uniforms and new instruments. Bedecked in new chaps, dusters, bandannas, and cowboy hats, starting in 1922, the Terry Cornbelt Band held weekly summer concerts at the town bandstand.

Origins of a Memorable Odyssey

The most famous event surrounding the Terry Corn-belt Band was their trip to the Black Hills of South Dakota to play at the summer white house of the 30th President of the U.S. Calvin Coolidge on July 4, 1927, a celebration of the President's 55th birthday. (Coolidge, a Republican, served as President from 1923-1929, and was first thrust into the position after President Warren G. Harding died unexpectedly while in office.)

According to the journals of band member Billy Grandfield, the Terry Cornbelt Band had just returned from Glendive where they had played at the celebration of the town and the opening of the branch line of the Northern Pacific Railroad to Circle-Brockway. During their stay in Glendive, band members were treated as guests of the officials of the NPRR in their private cars. Someone asked the question, "Where do we play next?"

One of the members, "in an off-hand manner," according to Grandfield, responded, "For President Coolidge's birthday!" Another voice chimed in, "Why not?" Another member of the band, W.R. Flachsenhar, a State Representative, parroted the question, "Why not?" Inspired, Flachsenhar wrote to Congressman Lovitt, and both men eventually corresponded directly with the President's secretary on the matter. Soon, a wire arrived with the President's invitation for the band to appear at the summer White House, which was about 35 miles from Rapid City, on July 4th at 1:30 p.m. According to Grandfield, "we held a practice meeting on that night and was ready to go next day making the start and on the way."

As a present for Coolidge, they chose a pair of chaps made by Al Furstnow's Saddlery, in Miles City. The original invoice shows the purchase price of "1 pr. Coolidge chaps" at $36.00, minus a "special reduction" of $8.50, for the billable total of $27.50.

Seventy-seven people packed in 22 vehicles and caravanned to the Black Hills, including a designated official car, a truck for instruments, and a chuck wagon. First stop, an evening of music in Fallon. The route then traversed through Mildred, Ismay, Baker, Camp Crook, South Dakota, and Buffalo, South Dakota.

Meeting President Coolidge

THE MORNING OF THE JULY 4TH visit, Grandfield wrote that some of the group "seemed a little excited on thought of meeting with the President and his Wife…But most of us old hands went about our tasks just like meeting with Presidents were an everyday thing with us."

The band marched past hundreds of people that lined the road on both sides until they came to the entrance to the White House lawn, when the sentry on duty stepped aside and stood at attention while they passed. They followed Colonel Edmund W. Starling up the driveway and onto the lawn where they formed a circle in concert formation. In a few moments the President and Mrs. Coolidge appeared, and the crowd and the band joined in a loud cheer. "We played a piece or two and the President came down on the lawn from the House," journaled Grandfield.

Colonel Starling motioned Rep Flachsenhar, who in behalf of "the Terry Montana Cowboy Band"—the band settled on the new moniker during the drive to the Black Hills—and the people of Montana, presented the President with the chaps of light-colored leather, embossed with silver studs around the edges and the letters CAL in silver down each leg, and a medallion monogram on the bottom of each leg, hand engraved, with the words Presented By The Terry Cowboy Band, above a picture of a cowboy riding a bucking bronco.

Rep Flachsenhar said a few chosen words that was received by the President "with a broad smile and a handshake." The Boy Scouts then came forward and presented the President with a horse, saddle, spurs, shirt and kerchief. Subsequently, a four-year-old from Terry named Frances Lillian Hewitt presented Mrs. Coolidge a beautiful bouquet of pink roses, and the Terry Montana Cowboy Band and friends received an introduction to the President and the First Lady in sight of thousands of people who lined the road and covered the hillside. After which the band played a few selections and a song was sung by Korse Johnson, the drum major, which "caused the President and his wife to smile." Afterwards, she approached Johnson and requested the words and music of the song be sent to her as soon as the band returned home. The president donned his cowboy rig, and the band played more tunes.

Soon, the White House servants arrived with loads of trays, and a large half-circle formed with the Cowboy Band in the center, and their families and friends from Montana on one side. After the birthday cake was unveiled, the band played another number or two, and the horse that was presented to

the President by the Boy Scouts was led into the circle, and the bridle reins was placed in the President's hands.

"Most everyone kept expecting to see the President mount his horse," wrote Grandfield. "But as he had not done much riding before he came to the Black Hills, he refrained from making any attempt to ride. But he led it around the lawn while the movie men took pictures..."

Coolidge cut his birthday cake and served it to his guests. At about 3 p.m. the President returned to the house and Mrs. Coolidge retired to the porch of the house overlooking the lawn "assured herself that everybody enjoyed themselves," recalled Grandfield. To conclude the memorable event, the Terry Montana Cowboy Band played several more numbers, saluted the observers, and marched away to camp.

Within a few hours, the band was embarking on the route to meet their next gig in Belle Fourche the following night.

Closing Stages of Terry Montana Cowboy Band

THE TERRY COWBOY BAND later made several other long journeys, including to Gallatin Gateway for the official opening of Yellowstone Park on June 29, 1929, the Minnesota State Fair in 1934, and the Golden Jubilee of the Montana Stockgrowers Association, also in 1934. The band too played at the celebration of the completion of the Northern Pacific Railroad between Glendive and Circle, playing a rousing set as the initial passenger train arrived in Circle, on June 2, 1928.

Newspaper clippings, photos and posters of the performances of the Terry Montana Cowboy Band may be found at the Prairie County Museum, in Terry. According to papers at the museum, the last documented event was a concert combining the Terry and Glendive bands in 1947 and the Terry Montana Cowboy Band officially ended in 1953. The chaps are now located in the Coolidge Room of the Forbes Library in Northampton, Massachusetts. Al Furstnow's Saddlery, in Miles City, operated in business from 1894 until 1982.

Boxer-Bricklayer Roger "The Opportunity Kid" Rouse

(1934-1999)

"You GOTTA BE TOUGH TO LIVE IN MONTANA." You hear it time and time again. Toughness epitomized the life of Roger Rouse. Indeed, Rouse might be the toughest—and greatest—athlete from Montana that most people today do not remember. Yes, even when *Sports Illustrated* compiled its list of the 50 greatest sports figures from Montana in 1999, Rouse failed to rank, although two other boxers, Marvin Camel (#18) and Todd Foster (#40), were included.

Of hardy Irish-Dutch stock, Rouse hailed from the industrial mining town of Opportunity, an unincorporated community in Deer Lodge County formed in the early 1900s by the Anaconda Copper Company. (Its current population stands at about 9,000 residents.) One of seven children of James and Mary Rouse, Roger found an opening with his brawn and boxing skills, competing for the world light heavyweight title twice.

Born on June 3, 1934, Roger Rouse started boxing at the age of 9 when his father, a smelterman at the Anaconda Copper Company, gave him and his younger brother Donald a pair of gloves for Christmas. In this, they learned the fundamentals from Nat Fleischer's *How to Box*. Fleischer, the founder of *Ring Magazine*, understood the principles of pugilism, and published his findings in 1929.

In a large feature that appeared in *Sports Illustrated* in 1967, Roger spun the questionable yarn that his "first formal instruction in boxing from a reformed alcoholic who was training fighters in the back of what is now the Wonder Bar." "He worked on my jab, started on my hook a little bit," Roger related to the popular magazine, "but then he wouldn't be there. He went on a drunk, picked up a deaf-and-dumb girl and got 50 years."

Nonetheless, Rouse boxed in high school at Anaconda, his coach, Jack Lodell, was the town's probation officer. A football standout and all-state fullback at Anaconda High School, as a teenager he also worked long, hot hours on a ranch, and rode competitively in the Jackpot Rodeo, in the wild horse race.

After being graduated from high school in 1953, Rouse enrolled at Idaho State College on a boxing scholarship. During his varsity career of 33 victories and 2 losses, he won the intercollegiate 165-pound championship twice. He won a Golden Gloves title in 1954 at Chicago, and after being graduated from Idaho State, he entered Montana State University on a football scholarship.

However, Rouse returned to boxing once more while recovering from a knee injury, and soon the violent lure of the padded ring overtook his desire for more education.

He was twice NCAA champion, and the 23-year-old athlete won a berth on the United States Olympic team which competed in Melbourne, Australia, in 1956, losing a highly disputed quarterfinal decision in Australia to Gilbert Chapron (1933-2016) of France because the judges said he was too rough.

Rouse turned professional in 1958, making his debut at the Cow Palace in Los Angeles, and eventually won the California State Light Heavyweight title, in 1964.

In his toughest match to date, Rouse fought Johnny Persol, a contender for the light heavyweight crown, at the Memorial Gym in Anaconda on November 23, 1964. The fight resulted in a first-round knockout for Rouse. Later in his career, Persol, whose face ended up looking like a Picasso painting, maintained that Rouse walloped him with such force that he suffered from "double vision" the rest of his career after a Rouse punch injured his orbital bone and detached his retina.

"Roger Rouse was a big celebrity in Anaconda at that time," says Chris Eamon, a friend and boxing protégé of Roger Rouse. "He was a country-boy type who never acted cocky. He loved to socialize, and Anaconda was hopping with bars and places to do it in the 1960s [one estimate says that in 1967 there were 37 bars within the city limits of Anaconda—perhaps more per capita than in any other city in the U.S.] He wasn't perfect but what you saw was what you got. He was as genuine as any person I have ever known."

Rouse vs. Tiger

As early as November 14, 1965, the *Independent Record* of Helena reported: Roger Rouse in a meteoric rise has climbed from virtual obscurity to a lofty position in the world light heavyweight realm and has already been ticketed for a shot at the title 'within the very near future'." After putting together a string of wins, he was graced with his biggest opportunity, designated the No. 1 light heavyweight contender in Novem-

ber, 1965. Two years later, on November 17, 1967, at slightly
over 174 pounds and 33-years-old, Roger Rouse challenged
the Republic of Biafra's 175-pound, 38-year-old world champion Dick Tiger for the World Boxing Council's World Light
Heavyweight title.

It would only the second time that a Montanan ever fought
for a world championship. In 1904 Jack Munroe, a Butte
prospector and part-time pugilist, met James J. Jeffries for the
heavyweight title in San Francisco; Munroe was knocked out
in the second round.

Approximately 1,000 people, including Governor Tim
Babcock traveled from Montana to Las Vegas to see Rouse,
nicknamed "The Opportunity Kid," get a crack at a world
title. Rouse, a standup fighter, with a fair jab and a decent left,
acquitted himself well in the first eight rounds, exhibiting his
good counterpunching skills. In the ninth round, however,
Tiger put Rouse down on the deck and took command of the
fight, battering Rouse, who was left bleeding from the face
and nose. Shortly into round twelve, Tiger floored Rouse to
end the fight.

Most of his career Rouse worked in a smelter in Anaconda
while he trained for bouts, employment set in scorching conditions where he shoveled tailings and welded steel. Inside the
ring his life was equally hazardous: In a fight in Las Vegas
against a guy named Eddie "Bossman" Jones in Las Vegas, in
May 1969, Rouse broke his hand.

Rouse vs. Foster

On April 4, 1970, Rouse challenged reigning champion Bob
Foster for Foster's light heavyweight title at the Henry Adams
Field House in Missoula. (Foster had won the World Boxing

Council's World Light Heavyweight title from Dick Tiger in 1968). Foster demolished Rouse with a vicious right hand, knocking the challenger down four times en route to a successful defense of his title. (Two years earlier, Foster also beat Rouse in a non-title bout.)

Bob Foster, dominant in the 175-pound division—he once held the division record for 14 successful title defenses—dispatched a number of top contenders in his career. Before Foster died in 2015, he was asked by *Ring Magazine*, who was the "pound for pound all-time hardest puncher" he had ever faced in the boxing ring, and he named Roger Rouse, "out of Montana."

"But he didn't look it, he didn't have the build or nothing," explained Foster. "He hit me on the chin in the first round, man, electricity started from my head, went all the way through my body down to my feet, my feet was on fire, man…I went back to the corner I said, 'What the hell did that son of a bitch hit me with?' I thought he hit me with a brick…but I busted him up, and beat him in the fifth round, they stopped the fight."

"Outside of the ring, Rouse, he was described as 'clean-cut' and 'modest.' He was one of a select group of fighters graduated from college. 'Shucks' and 'shoot' are the strongest expletives in Rouse's vocabulary…He is soft-spoken with a slow mid-western burr. A handsome lad, he looks more like a banker or lawyer than a boxer," said the July 1967 issue of *Boxing Illustrated*. Still, Rouse was no stranger to local bars and certainly not to trouble: the June before he was set to challenge Bob Foster for the light heavyweight champion, Roger and his younger brother, Donald, once a college light heavyweight boxer, were arrested on charges stemming from incidents in Butte. Police alleged the brothers were fighting in an alley but "joined forces" against police who arrested them after a new fight broke out in which two officers were injured. According to police, the Rouse brothers offered further resistance after being booked at the Butte City Jail.

"Roger is an extremist," once commented his trainer Pete Jovanovich to *Ring Magazine*. "Drink, fight, chase. As he once told me, 'If I wasn't the sonofabitch I am, I wouldn't be a fighter.' If you tame him out of the ring, you tame him in."

Death, Legacy of Smelter City Boxer

ONCE THE NO. 1 ranked light heavyweight around, the fall from grace since Rouse was KO'd by Dick Tiger was steep. From then on Rouse lost a lot in a relatively short period of time. After 66 career bouts and a string of nine consecutive losses held in such far-flung places as Johannesburg, South Africa, and Cologne, West Germany, Roger Rouse hung up his ring trunks and boxing gloves after tallying a 39-23-4 record. He retired from boxing in 1972 and worked at the Anaconda Co. Smelter in Anaconda until it closed in 1980. And on top of this, he coached the Anaconda Police Athletic League boxing team for several years.

On Sunday, March 7, 1999, the former light heavyweight boxer from the shining mountains died of Alzheimer's at the age of 64, at his Helena residence.

Not since the days of Joe Simonich and Dixie LaHood fighting in Butte in the 1920s and Ennis-born Hubert "Kid" Dennis and Missoula featherweight Ritchie Fontaine in the 1930s had Montana been so enthusiastic over a boxer who could have won a world championship. It boasted such a man in the Smelter City's light heavyweight Roger Rouse.

"He loved the people, the area, and the simple life," says Chris Eamon. "There is no telling how far he would have gone under big time management in a boxing Mecca like New York or Las

Vegas, but that wasn't his style. He was an easy-going guy that loved the small town and winning for hometown fans."

Elizabeth Clare Prophet

(1939-2009)

New Age Prophet in Paradise

Scripture commanded Elizabeth Clare Prophet to head for the mountains. As it turns out, Montana became the ideal destination.

And at the zenith of her influence, she was revered by thousands of people around the world as a spiritual leader who possessed a direct connection to God. Her supporters venerated her with a host of monikers: Mother, Guru Ma, Mother of the Flame and the Vicar of Christ.

Falls in Love; Founds Her Own Church Sect

Born in New Jersey as Elizabeth Clare Wulf, her life changed dramatically after she fell in love with Mark Prophet, a self-proclaimed messenger of God who found notoriety in the late 1950s as a fringe religious leader.

In 1975, Elizabeth founded the New Age sect called the Church Universal and Triumphant (CUT) shortly after the death of Mark, the founder of The Summit Lighthouse, a similar, earlier incarnation of CUT.

Elizabeth borrowed ideas from Buddhism, Hinduism and Kabbalah, and mixed them with the beliefs of a 1930s group known as the "I AM" Religious Activity that used chanted decrees. She wrote a number of books, a few of them exclusively about her and her church, and "could preach for hours and never break a sweat," according to one account.

According to CUT doctrine, Elizabeth was a courier, a direct link to God who could take dictations from Ascended Masters, heavenly idols ranging from Buddha to Jesus to Pope John Paul XXIII to the "head of the Cosmic Secret Service." A messenger such as Elizabeth was the one person on earth worthy or capable of channeling such interpretation.

Church Sets Up Puritanical Ranch; Predicts Armageddon

In 1981, when CUT first arrived in the Paradise Valley and bought the Royal Teton Ranch, publisher John Sullivan urged readers of the *Livingston Enterprise* to adopt a "wait and see" attitude about the group, which, according to one interpretation, offered up "a mixture of right-wing politics, reincarnation theory and survivalism."

By the mid-1980s, church members set up the central

complex of their religious community in Corwin Springs, north of Gardiner, disavowing smoking, alcohol consumption, and illegal drugs, as well as condemning homosexuality and premarital sex. Moreover, some of the prohibitions were even more restrictive, according to one Associated Press writer: "The church frowns on most forms of modern music, like rock 'n' roll, blues or jazz, which it considers destructive and anti-family."

Prophet said that she received messages from the Creator that indicated that the struggle between the forces of freedom and godless totalitarianism was about to devolve into an all-out war, with the United States and President Ronald Reagan representing the former, and the Soviet Union, or "the Evil Empire," as Reagan once dubbed it, the manifestation of the latter.

"The church is staunchly anti-communist and anti-Soviet Union, supports President Reagan's strategic defense initiative and pushes for a nationwide civil-defense system," reported the Associated Press.

Ultimately, Prophet began telling her followers that the end of days would come in 1990 when a nuclear war would erupt between the two powerful nations.

"I think Americans are totally unprepared psychologically for any disaster or war," Prophet once said. "They haven't seen it. And they don't believe they can survive a nuclear war. The Soviets believe they can survive a nuclear war."

Bulldozed Land; Constructed Bunkers

PEOPLE MOVED TO THE COMPOUND from all over the US and world. Prophet said that members of the CUT weren't simply a band of puritanical vigilantes, but represented a broad cross-section of American society: some were aimless and drifting; some were noble and educated; some were high school dropouts; some were older vagabonds, who had experienced the ways of the world; and still some were barely out of their teens, on a validating quest for their identities.

Members brought their money with them and handed it over to the church. When former church members described the church as a manipulative cult that practiced "authoritarian mind control," Prophet voiced objections. When they claimed that she was constructing a bomb shelter on church land, she said that there were only a few "transformed basements."

But when the bulldozers and heavy equipment arrived to plow, rip apart, and fortify the 33,000 acres of the fragile ecology of the Gallatin Range, local environmentalists ignited a bitter dispute. When one of the tanks leaked 31,000 gallons of diesel oil and gasoline that endangered a spawning area creek for cutthroat trout that supplies the Yellowstone River, their fears proved well warranted.

Many locals were less concerned with the environmental repercussions or even the idiosyncratic religious logic of the group's doctrine, and more worried about the implications of what appeared to be some sort of survivalist compound. Replete with a concrete-and-steel gun tower with machine gun slits and massive 750-person bomb shelter, the area in question was constructed at the center of the CUT complex.

Critics feared the Prophet was the female repeat of Peoples Temple founder Jim Jones. On November 18, 1978, Jones led hundreds of his followers—the final death count was 909; a third of those who committed suicide or were shot were children—in a mass murder-suicide at their agricultural commune in a remote section of the South American nation of Guyana. Jones, an avowed Marxist, bamboozled the people with utopian gibberish and influence-peddling social programs and mind and language control.

Worries that the cult was preparing for its own violent, divinely inspired version of Armageddon were heightened in July 1989 when Prophet's fourth husband, Edward Francis, was convicted of using an assumed name to attempt to purchase $150,000 worth of high-powered weaponry. (At one point the church had as many as 600 employees; Francis outlined plans to arm and train an army of 200 people.)

Her Influence Has Faded; Yet Followers Remain

ELIZABETH CLARE PROPHET departed from the public view after she announced her dementia Alzheimer's disease diagnosis in 1999, at the age of 59. By that time most of Prophet's five children had openly denounced their mother's activities. (Her fifth child, Seth, was born when Elizabeth was 55 years old and still wed to a man who wasn't the newborn boy's father. She was married four times.)

Son Sean Prophet told the *Bozeman Daily Chronicle* in 2005 that the church of youth "reeked of fundamentalism" and imposed "near-Taliban style restrictions on dress and human interaction." Daughter Tatiana believed there were some upsides to her mother's preaching, but that there was negativity that the church supported that dwarfed the good, specifically, she said, "the whole idea that a nuclear attack could be eminent" and the "quite-loopy political views."

Despite such ostracism, until her death in 2009, Elizabeth affirmed that she was the sole and only living messenger of the CUT and never hesitated to remind others of her divine virtuosity and select company. An alarmingly frail and emaciated Prophet would occasionally make an appearance off the compound in part to squelch rumors that she had died or had given up supremacy over the minions. Other spiritual figures from the past designated to be special messengers by the CUT, she was quick to note, included 17th Century French alchemist Saint Germain and William Shakespeare.

In the 1990s, a number of church officials defected from the organization. Around that time, the U.S. Forest Service purchased about half of the church's Royal Teton Ranch. On the other half, the Church Universal and Triumphant still holds summits and spiritual retreats, all dedicated to keeping the message of Elizabeth Clare Prophet's revelations cherished and propagated.

Bruce Vorhauer

(1941-1992)

No Man Is A 'Sponge' Island

BRUCE WARD VORHAUER built a fortune on the contraceptive sponge. But riches soon gave way to bankruptcy, political defeat and tragedy. At the end, he wound up a paranoid, frightened, lonely, frustrated ex-millionaire who had gotten too big for his britches and couldn't cope with the failure.

Sitting Pretty on Contraception Investment

THE SON OF AN AIRPLANE repairman and a secretary, Vorhauer grew up in Virginia and worked his way to engineering, biomedical and business degrees. He wound up as director of research and development for American Hospital Supply Corporation, working out of its Irvine, California, offices.

His job brought him in contact with a professor who was working on the concept that "sponge-like material could be impregnated with spermicide" and used as a vaginal contraceptive. When other investors and companies rejected the idea, Vorhauer decided to support it.

In 1975, he borrowed the sum of $400,000 from an investor, enough to buy the patent on the professor's sponge. Then he began the seven-year march toward Food and Drug Administration approval.

Ultimately, Vorhauer Laboratories Inc., later VLI Corp., introduced the first new contraceptive technology in decades, and its Today sponge became the most popular over-the-counter contraceptive for women.

Just after the sponge received FDA approval to go on the market, Vorhauer was featured in *Forbes* magazine.

"At 41, Vorhauer is sitting pretty," *Forbes* declared. "Though his stake in the company lately has been diluted to 11%, it's still worth about $4 million at prices set by the latest private financing. When VLI goes public, that stake will be worth far more."

Vorhauer, "handsome, well-spoken and admired," according to another magazine profile about him, took to his new wealth with rabid intensity. In 1983, when VLI went public, Vorhauer sold some of his stock and got his initial taste of the wealth he had envisioned. Soon he was whooping it up, oblivious that his fortunes had peaked.

Riches and Setbacks

THE HINDRANCES BEGAN in December, 1983. Only six months after the Today contraceptive sponge went on the market, a news report connected the sponge and toxic shock syndrome, a potentially lethal ailment previously linked to certain tampons. The reports turned out to be unsupported, but sales and stock value plummeted.

Then in October, 1984, Vorhauer, driving on an icy road in Montana, skidded broadside into a tree, critically injuring his fiancée, Sara Wright. She died in a coma eight months later. Vorhauer took a six-month leave from VLI.

In 1987, Vorhauer began to rebuke the top managers he had brought into the company. By then, VLI stock had fallen from its euphoric high of 26 just after going public to its rock bottom of 3. Although 75 million Today sponges had been sold, the company had yet to show a profit.

More stumbling blocks. In July, 1987, as American Home Products was negotiating to buy the company, VLI lost the patent on the Today contraceptive sponge because it had neglected to pay a $150 patent maintenance fee. VLI would eventually reclaim its patent, but in the interim, VLI's selling price was chopped down by $9.5 million.

That still netted Vorhauer an estimated $3.75 million. In all, he reaped between $5 million and $7 million from VLI, according to one estimate. He captured the money and went to Montana to stay.

Creation of "Sponge Island"

HE BUILT A MANSION in the middle of Salmon Lake on Sourdough Island, known derisively by locals as "Sponge Island," a 17,000-square-foot oasis that dwarfed everything else. He decorated with art works—about $500,000 worth, according to his bankruptcy declaration.

Still obsessed with climbing the ladder, he invested in real estate, in a hotel and in fledgling biomedical companies that he expected to build and sell at great profit, as he had with VLI.

To Vorhauer—who had long harbored political aspirations as a means of status—Montana must have looked like the Promised Land. By 1989, Vorhauer was traveling in Montana political circles, preparing for a run at the U.S. Senate. He apparently was not discouraged by his tightening financial predicament. He continued spending heavily, taking out the first of a series of loans that would eventually bring him to bankruptcy.

Vorhauer announced his candidacy in January, 1990, and started his campaign for the Republican nomination. Around that time, he asked Democratic Sen. Max Baucus and the state's two Republican congressmen to pull some strings in an attempt to secure an ambassador's post in Southeast Asia. State Department officials, however, declined to offer Vorhauer any posts. "Any Southeast Asian country would do," Vorhauer said to Baucus.

Vorhauer's pro-choice stand on abortion differed from most of his Republican colleagues, who supported a constitutional amendment to prohibit abortions. He said that he opposed any law "infringing on the right of a woman to have an abortion."

He lost the Senate bid, drawing 35% of the vote, and was left with $168,847 in campaign debts. And on top of this, Vince and Joan Wright filed a lawsuit against him for the wrongful death of their daughter and his fiancée, Sarah, and he was forced to make amends.

Creditors were swarming. To raise money, he attempted to sell his mansion, first for $7.5 million, and then he dropped the asking price to $5.5 million. There were no buyers. His yacht in Seattle went on the market. No takers, either.

This reality became untenable for him.

A Cocktail of Defaults, Repossession, Arson, Suicide

VORHAUER HAD GONE from being "the golden boy" whose personal income fell from $3.3 million in 1987 to $60,000 in only four years at a time when he owed more than $300,000 a year in interest alone.

He defaulted on loans, forcing longtime friends to pay $600,000 on a note they had guaranteed. On Thursday, May 30, 1991, Vorhauer received a phone call from an attorney who told him that unless Vorhauer paid the more than $1 million he owed on his yacht within 24 hours, it would be repossessed the following Monday. Vorhauer could no longer borrow even modest sums of money.

Desperate, he drove to Seattle.

On Sunday, June 2, the day before the repossession, Vorhauer's yacht burned to the waterline. He told fire investigators that he had tried to "repair a heat exchanger in a stateroom closet with a propane torch," according to insurance records. He said he left the boat with the torch apparently still on.

He filed an insurance claim for $1.3 million, and the insurance company was about to fork over the check. But the claims manager gave the file to fraud investigators for a final opinion before paying. They determined that his story just didn't make sense.

In September, 1992, a judge ruled that the fire was arson and freed the insurance company from obligation to pay. Seattle fire investigators then took their evidence to the county prosecutor's office. According to news accounts, prosecutors had tentatively decided to file arson charges against Vorhauer. Although no one had officially notified him, he most likely knew of the criminal investigation.

Then on September 21, less than three weeks after the insurance judgment and the day before his Montana mansion was to be sold at sheriff's auction, Vorhauer filed for bankruptcy.

Ten days later, on October 1, 1992, he drove to the edge of the lake where his house was built and killed himself. With bankruptcy, defaulted loans, an arson investigation and fraud hanging over him, he could handle no more and saw no escape. He left a note reportedly confirming that he'd died by his own hand and professing love for his wife, Charlotte, and two sons.

The man who'd always projected the image of himself as the idealistic genius, the creative entrepreneur, the golden boy of the family, the success, he was dead at 50, and by his own hand. He'd run a hose from his car's exhaust pipe and breathed the fumes until he gave up the ghost.

Tim Dobbie, one of his former partners, had this to say of the mercurial inventor after learning of the suicide: "I never understood the guy. You want to understand him? Good luck."

Now known as Montana Island Lodge, the mansion was donated to the University of Montana by philanthropist Denny Washington, who acquired the property to satisfy debts against Vorhauer, and the college utilizes the property as a resort and corporate retreat.

A GALLERY OF PRESENT-DAY ECCENTRICS

Raymond Ansotegui

Bullfighter, Cowboy Protector

Bullfighters are not rodeo clowns. Bullfighters function with an almost primal sense of principle: serve as a human shield for bull riders who've been chucked or thrown from bulls after their eight-second rides.

Call the bullfighter's job a perilous game of tag. Call it the most serious part of the rodeo world. Call it anything but clowning around. Indeed, the bullfighter no longer dresses up like a clown to risk life and limb.

"I don't wear face paint, baggy pants or any torn-out shorts or suspenders," said Raymond Ansotegui (whose Basque name is pronounced an-SOH´-tuh-ghee).

Equipped with a chest plate, a back plate, a rib guard, shorts snug with padding in the legs and back, and a pair of cleats, Ansotegui subverts bulls in a battle of gripping, meaningful unease.

"I don't wear knee braces, but I've got a sports jersey and a cowboy hat," said Ansotegui. "I'm not worried about not being protected. The more gear you wear, the slower you are going to be."

Every millisecond is precious in an enclosed arena where reflexes lightning-fast and impeccable timing can be the difference between life and serious injury. Perhaps no job provides a jolt of clarity fiercer than the one the bullfighter contacts. Being kicked, bumped or trampled by a bull is the wake-up call.

"You are going to take a shot and you have to take one shot every now and again to see what's in you and what it is you are made of," said Ansotegui.

Still, no matter how prepared for harm he may be, before a

night of dodging bulls, Ansotegui is suitably nervy with anxiety. He goes into survival mode, mentally withdrawing into a private world which requires sharp focus and unique biomechanics.

"I'm not an adrenaline junkie. You know, the first time in the arena, once the gate latches shut, it's like a tornado. But then it gets really calm. You are always nervous, but your brain is in a different place. There has to be some nerves going for me, or someone may get hurt."

Ansotegui's work starts before the cowboy hits the dirt. He has to react while allowing himself enough time to assess, control and manage the situation. Literally getting on the bull's bad side is part of his job, and he must move with slick, smart panache.

Bullfighting is a rescue of inches. The game plan that he's relied on since he began bullfighting six years ago is simple: You have to hurl your body in the action.

"People come off in bad spots, and you have to come in through the tightest of space, essentially between the bull and the rider. And you can get so tight that you have one hand on each of them—one hand on the bull, and the other on the rider, touching them both. There is not a lot of space, and sometimes there is no space. You get close enough to feel the hooves and snot of the bull."

If he times his diversionary entrance and exit perfectly, the cowboy has a few precious seconds to scamper to safety and the bull's absorbed attention is either focused on the opposite direction or locked on him.

"Don't run in a straight line," said Ansotegui. "That's not easy. You can spin faster than the bull can. But they can push you out of the way, catch you, and give you a love tap. I guess it's a love tap to them. But you end up eight feet in the air, and in your mind, you are thinking, 'dammit, this is going to hurt when I come down.' It is like having a dancing partner who doesn't want to do the same moves as you. With your hand on the bull, you are controlling the situation, walking where you want to go. Something is pretty cool about that feeling."

Raymond studied at the bullfighting school of Al Sandvold, a North Dakota-born cowboy living in Belgrade. "Al taught me that the bullfighter has to be quiet and quick, not flashy, and that his job is to keep cowboys safe and have his shit together."

Sandvold taught Raymond how to read the body language of the rider, sensing, feeling, speculating the very second he will need to act in the role of cowboy protector.

"I have to be able to see if the cowboy is going to come off," said Ansotegui. "I can see his hips shift or other indicators. I have an advantage if I can start early, if I can get to the gap early. You can see the cowboy rock out or see his hips shake the wrong way, off to the side of the bull. Unless he makes a move and corrects, he is getting tossed. You see that the cowboy's feet come too close to his mid-core, and they have no more grip. When you see the boot and spur in the high area, you know there is a good chance he is coming off or going over the bull's head."

Bulls have ranging temperaments and Ansotegui, who holds a master's degree in Reclamation from Arizona State University, has spent ample time working with and studying cows. His father worked as an animal science professor at Montana State University and Raymond spent many of his summers helping him conduct field research.

"I've always found it fascinating, the interaction with a large animal," said Ansotegui. "When bullfighting, you know which ones are the meanest, and, even with the meanest, once they are done, they go in the back and they are calm."

Similar to all other professions, the bullfighter has good days and bad days. A few months ago, Raymond took a pounding from the first bull of the night. He needed to regroup fast. He had to safely protect more than two dozen other riders.

"The first bull came out and he got a hold of me. He got me in a bad spot and gave me a couple of shots. That was the first bull of the day and I fought 28 or 29 others that night. But you need to remember that you came to protect. And you don't want to give the thirtieth guy less protection. It is not fun to get freight trained. You are sore. You are busted up. But you just can't wait to go do it again."

Ansotegui said that working as a bullfighter has provided him with a renewed sense of respect for the fact-moving action.

"I love watching the guys ride bulls and to see the partnership with riders and bulls. There is no better seat in the house to see the power and motion between two things."

The bullfighter's job is to take a "love tap" from the bull, like the Secret Service leaps in front of a bullet for the president. Your average bullfighter, though, has saved more lives than your typical agent in the Secret Service. Cowboys, with one or two rides a night, grace newspapers and television high-lights. Bullfighters—who work in pairs—are just in the back-ground, an understated, integral piece of the puzzle. There is no such thing as crazy when describing bullfighting—it's a tightly choreographed performance of ballet, bulls, and pure balls. In fact, Raymond talks mundanely about preparing for events by drinking plenty of water and stocking up on ice packs, and the importance of a healthy diet, ample exercise, and, if possible, resting wounds.

"You can't come to the battle if you haven't prepared," he said.

Unremitting curiosity can often stir a bit of havoc on the emotional lives of men. Raymond answered his own curios-ity and started working as a bullfighter at age 34. He under-stands that his body is going to take a pounding, and plans to keep evading bulls at least a few more years. "At 40, you know when you take a good muscle shot that it'll be sore for a while. It needs a little more time to rehab."

Ansotegui is an amateur bullfighter; the Professional Rodeo Cowboys Association, a wider circuit encompassing the entire sport, puts on approximately 1,000 pro rodeos annually. Roughly 300 men work as bullfighters, only about one-tenth of them make it a full-time living. Bullfighters have to be selected to advance.

"Every time you show up to work you are earning your invi-tation to your next gig," said Ansotegui. "Maybe I could have gone further if I had started earlier. But, you know, I'm not the most athletic guy in the world. But there was something I just needed to prove to myself."

Most of his assignments come through the Roughrider Rodeo Association, with the bulk of the events in Montana, North Dakota, and Canada. And it's not just the bullriders who work their way up; the bulls end up on different levels, too.

"It's not unusual to see one of the bulls you just faced on television two or three weeks later at a professional event," said Ansotegui, who lives in Livingston and works at John Deere in sales.

No matter the level, the threat of being hurt or maimed by a striking bull is his occupational reality. Bottom line: He's ready to die for riders every time.

"If I make enough to cover my travel, lodging, and food, and I have some money left over, I'm perfect. More than that is, I get a bunch of memories of knowing that I did everything I could to keep everyone safe."

Jem Blueher

The Wheels Just Keep Turning For
Livingston Anvil Worker

WORKING ON HIS OWN at Livingston Anvil Works, Jem Blueher is something of a rebel. Backed by the might of aged, gritty
equipment, he restores rare horse-drawn vehicles, tools, and
machinery through rigorous application.

Perhaps not surprisingly, he also hates to throw old-fash-
ioned stuff away.

There is an original wooden buggy body that he uses as shelf
space attached to one of the shop walls. He's surrounded by
the tonnage of 20th-century industrial machinery, as well as
sets of German and Japanese cannon wheels, various boxes of
wooden slats, reconditioned tools from the 1850s and the shells
and fragmented scraps of old touring coaches.

"I think the interest in restoration started when I used to do
small repair jobs with my stepdad," said Jem Blueher. "He's
an old cowboy from Great Falls, and when he was growing up
it was all was horse-drawn, and the equipment was old. We'd
pick up old wagons and do restoration on sheep wagons and
covered wagons. It was a lot more fun than the electrical engineering work I was doing."

Raised in Livingston, Blueher started working in restoration while in his mid-20s. A mixture of self-resolve, adaptabil-
ity, and external economic forces pushed him along his life's
path. "I'd went down to Denver and there were huge layoffs
of the engineering work force and a massive amount of experienced people around, and it was hard to get work," he said. "I
took some engineering temp jobs for a few years, and I hated

160

being inside. I went AWOL in Alaska as a river guide and then back to Colorado and worked in the mountains as ski instructor and river guide. Then it was back to Livingston, working with log homes. My stepdad got sick, and I helped him out with that (restoration work). We manufactured teepees and canvas goods."

Perhaps all that can be said about Blueher's conversion to business is that there were many self-determined factors at work that gradually and steadily led him to this current moment.

"Most of my learning came from conferences, talking to blacksmiths and taking clinics," Blueher said. "I tracked down people who did upholstery, those people are becoming less and less." Indeed, from sheep wagons and chuck wagons to covered wagons and stagecoaches, to buggies, carriages, sleighs and even Civil War-era cannons, Blueher can unwrap the mystery of refurbishment through bold trial and error and by locating adequate explanations from sources whose knowledge is often difficult to access.

When a problem or glitch leaves his head spinning, Blueher reminds himself that restoration work is rife with the sort of issues that evoke no simple answer. The vagaries of experimentation and patience clear his head and center his focus.

"Often I don't know how to get to the end of the project," said Blueher, 52. "So you start trying different things and you get it done. It's about not being afraid to start and to go for it." In Blueher's world, true freedom of self-employment cannot be an aimless drifting in the realms of casualness or the unsystematic. Such liberty of labor has to be compatible with study, resolve, and perhaps most importantly, knowledge.

"I get to do hands-on research and that's cool," said Blueher. "I'll see when it was made and tracking down the serial numbers and looking into the blacksmith stamp. I was working

on an English-style enclosed coach and pulled out its uphol-
stering, which was wrecked and mouse-ridden, and there was
an old calling card of the original owner. Somehow it was a
descendant of royalty in Europe and the family ended up as
a Confederate family who ran their home as a hospital in the
Civil War. The estate is still in the same family."

As with most occupations, parts of it are fulfilling and other
parts are dreary. "I love to have any excuse to play on the forge,"
he said. "I love building bodies and the wheelwrighting. Sandblasting is not fun or glamorous, but it has to be done. Strip-
ping paint is tedious. But then I'll start building again and
that's where it starts to get exciting."

Livingston Anvil Works has shipped covered wagons to Florida, Georgia, Michigan and other states, though most of his
orders came from the West. Sometime ago, he even shipped a
pair of covered wagons to Japan. His clients range from private
collectors and dude ranches to those wishing to preserve family
heirlooms. Currently, Blueher is immersed in refurbishing an
Abbot-Downing Yellowstone Touring stagecoach, which he
concedes is a "big project," even by his standards. The last time
he worked on one of similar vintage, he put in close to 700
hours—nearly four months of labor.

"It's as much about bringing things to life as it is keeping to the
old tradition," he said. "Tearing things apart, you are constantly
learning from the old tradesmen just by re-engineering."

While the businessman in Blueher has a vision of reality
which is clear, the sentimental artisan within holds a perspective on life that is more balanced. "It's hard to part with them,
just like a baby. When I drop it (a carriage or buggy or other
restoration) off, it always feels weird. When they are driving off
with it, I'm always wondering if it is tied down well enough,
and I hope they take care of it."

Chip Clawson

A Ceramicist's Backyard Visions

CERAMICIST AND ARCHIE BRAY constituent Chip Clawson started throwing functional pots while he was a college undergraduate in 1966. A few years later, he was employed as a professional studio potter in Edinboro, Pennsylvania.

His well-worn origin story is less important than its persistence or its aptness or its uncanny economy. Hands immersed in the clay, something inside of him bubbled up in an irrepressible effervescence. Pottery was a new outlook and a new sense of power, a mode of taking the reins on his own terms.

"While I was in college," explained Chip, "I was living with a friend who was an art major, and in the evenings, I was in the studio exchanging time for mixing clay. I learned basic throwing and then I went into the Marine Corps. I didn't want to be an air traffic controller after the service. Honestly, nothing comes too easy for me. But clay did come easy. Soon, I was making pots and giving it a go out of an old garage."

From 1975-1977, Clawson worked as the ceramics studio technician at the University of Michigan. Clawson realized the voyager's life in Montana after he received an introduction to it from his friend Kurt Weiser, who had recently been named the director of the Archie Bray Foundation for the Ceramic Arts.

The day that realization dawned on him was one of the greatest, if not the greatest, of his life.

"I came out in March 1977, and it was 40 degrees here and dry and I had just left a cold Chinook in Michigan, and pretty soon I had seen two mountain goats along the skyline,

and that sealed the deal, and I fell in love with Montana. Since then, the mountain goat has become my totem. I chose not to go back East. Recreation, beauty, and a low population density drew me here."

Resident artists Rudy Autio and Peter Voulkos were part of the original pottery building dedication at the Bray in 1951. But the organization slid into bankruptcy in 1960 and almost everyone except a couple of intense potters working out of a converted chicken coop had headed elsewhere. In 1966 potter David Shaner purchased an acre and a half of property on behalf of the newly minted Archie Bray Foundation for the Ceramic Arts. In the mid-1980s Clawson and several others negotiated to acquire the original brickyard, and that purchase subsequently changed the entire scope of the organization. These days the Bray is noted for its artist-in-residence programs, drawing ceramicists from around the world.

Clawson served from 1977 to 2004 as its clay business manager and from 2009-2014 as the facilities manager.

"The Archie Bray today is a vibrant, fiscally sound organization," said Clawson, flooded by emotion. "I'm proud to say that I have even been a part of that. Though I've retired from there for the third and final time, my fingerprints are out there. It's a special place to me, where I've spent around 36 years out of the 41 years I've been here."

Additionally, Clawson has constructed several public art projects, including a couple of installations in Billings at the Montana Women's Prison and a low-income apartment complex.

Since 1998 he has been imparting layers of impulsive finesse in the backyard of his Helena home, a widening investiture of spiraled concrete columns pressed with random coats of tiny earthenware. Heavily influenced by Spanish architect Antoni Gaudi (1852–1926) and Edward James (1907-1984), a British poet known for his patronage of the surrealist art movement, Clawson delights in the constructs of his own whims. Another of Clawson's most direct influences, Henry Chapman Mercer (1856-1930), was a major proponent of the Arts & Crafts movement in America who used tiles and mosaics in innovative fashions.

By playing the game of inspiration his way, Clawson lets his passion speak for itself. Indeed, the backyard visionary in him is perennially developing prototypes. Works merge clay, concrete and other materials. Concrete is the property's most significant structural and visual element; ceramics are a smaller decorative part of the equation.

"Art in the natural world, the living world is a big influence for me. This kind of art, in my own home and my own environment, allows me to express what's coming out of me and is tied in to where I am going. I draw inspiration from the natural, man-made and site-specific worlds."

Clawson's innovative endeavors may also be seen locally at Pioneer Park, the Archie Bray, the Jefferson School (Buddy Benches), and the Fish Bench (Biggo) at the Great Northern Town Center. After Biggo was smashed in its nose in the spring of 2017, Clawson repaired the installation with matching pieces and fits. But in the summer of 2018, the installation's prominent convex surface was vandalized much more extensively.

"It's disappointing to me (the vandalism)," said Clawson. "I used to believe that graffiti was the primary concern, and this may be naive and ill-informed, but I believed that some respect was out there for public art."

Despite the random acts of defacement, Clawson said that the majority of people cling to a cherished view of public art and appreciate its manifold visual, emotional and communal residuals.

"I get so much feedback from the community at the carousel about Biggo, especially with people and their children or grandchildren. I get a lot of feedback on it, and I like the work that I've done here."

At 75, art even now provides Clawson with stirring testimony and extensive new research. He spends his winter time constructing forms in the four kilns that he operates in a Boulder Avenue studio. His endlessly evolving built environment provides him with a functioning mentality that's driven less by dramatic necessity than it is by the urgency to tap and utilize inner powers.

"I don't have to answer to anyone at this point," said Clawson. "I mean, the only thing that limits me is my own ability and my own imagination, and that's quite a gift. Fortunately, my neighbors like living with it, which is good because it is becoming more and more prominent in their lives. I'm building stuff, and I need to do that, and I can do it."

Reflecting on the ceramicist's life, Clawson said that the beauty of art is that it has never tried to force an answer upon him, but it has kept him calm and sharp, as well as allowed him to assemble a life impartially and judicially.

"Art has allowed me to live in Montana, and the work that I did was something that did more than only provide me with a paycheck."

Chip Clawson's outdoor sculpture environment may be viewed at 202 Pine Street, Helena, Montana.

Troy "Good Medicine" De Roche

Hot Springs, MT

Playing, Making Flutes From The Heart

Troy De Roche has long equated the flute with the patina of positivity.

The Blackfeet flautist, 64, was born on the Flathead Indian Reservation on the edge of a Heart Butte cattle ranch. In the spring, grandfather would use his pocket knife to slice and yank the chips off of the cedar trees. He'd proceed to poke out holes in the bark, carving it like a whistle.

"After they were dried out, they would last for a day or so as crude flutes," said De Roche. "That's what got me interested."

The flute re-emerged in De Roche's life many years later, this time materializing as the choice between self-creation or self-destruction. His life was at a dead end. In the late-1980s, De Roche, smarting from the effects of back surgery from a work-related injury and a broken neck sustained in a car crash, grabbed a shaving of western red cedar and carved his nephew a flute. He made himself one, too. Memories of willow bark flutes fashioned by his grandfather's hands abetted his recovery.

"I blew out three lower vertebrae working in construction on the Blackfeet reservation," said De Roche. "They were always sideways. By the time I'd take the one-hour drive back home from the doctor's office, they'd be back out again.

"I don't believe there is anything more healing than going through therapy with a flute or playing the flute. Once I'd had the flute back in my life, I quit drinking and doing drugs, and I am blessed that I got into flute. It has changed my life and changed my attitude on life."

Constructing flutes crystallized an about-face; realizing that he had to stop being a slave to dependency and self-pity, De Roche felt autonomy at his fingertips. The old ways with which he struggled for so long disappeared. What replaced them were new pathways sparked by the jubilant sounds and scents of cedar. Intuiting that De Roche was embarking on a special path, Browning elder Al Potts even gave him the name "Shu'k Sha'mii," or "Good Medicine."

De Roche creates flutes inside a garage adjacent to his gallery in Hot Springs, Montana. There, with a routing tool, adhesive, clamps, and the dexterity of his hands, he takes a cudgel of wood and transforms it into the epitome of pure beauty in sound. Before one of his flutes is complete, he will wet sand it three times with fine sandpiper; its maintenance no more than the occasional lathering of beeswax.

"Cedar is one of the main woods I use because it's a soft wood and the grain is straight," said De Roche. "I split it and then carve it out and then glue it back together. Western red cedar has a softer, mellow earthy tone. Aromatic cedar, which is in the juniper family, is sweet with a perfume smell, and has a beautiful mellow tone.

"A lot of the woods out there are poisonous, especially the South American ones, so you don't want to be putting them in your mouth. Even still, often someone will say to me, 'I am going to get a wood shop, get a book, and make a flute.' I've never had any of those guys who say that ever come and bring a flute back. Because I still am learning stuff all of the time about making the flutes. If you angle them too much, they sound airy, if they are not angled enough, they sound airy."

Akin to the way that different woods produce special tones, inaccurately spaced or misaligned measurements can toss a flute grossly out of tune. The tricky thing about a flute is that if it's constructed out of tune, it simply can't be returned to be re-tuned. It's either clear-toned or it's not.

"I will pick up the flutes in the galleries and maybe one of twelve are in tune and playable, and I got tired of that," said De Roche. "If I won't get up on stage and play them, I won't sell them. Each wood is different. It was a living thing and to me it's still living. The first note out of the flute brings it back to life. It's an amazing feeling—like giving birth or life. To hear the beautiful tone that comes out after you make it, and the amazing music that comes out, is such a pleasure. A gift has been given to me to do this."

Give with all your heart and you will receive: De Roche's performances at festivals nationwide and five albums of original compositions have secured his reputation as an authentic conduit "of Native American people through music," he said. Indeed, preserving tradition and the nearly spectral resonance of the flute are important to De Roche. So, too, is gratitude.

"The first professional studio I worked in was in England and to go from a construction worker to a studio where the Beatles recorded was one of those great moments."

De Roche said that the natural sounds of the flute resonate on multiple ecological dimensions.

"It is such a healing thing for people to sit and play or listen to the flute," said De Roche. "There are times that I'll start playing and there are animals that will come on over. I was up by Bull Lake, by the giant cedars at a campground, and two loons were out on the lake. I took that flute and made the loon sound. The loons quit singing and looked over and they started answering in the middle of the lake."

De Roche speaks with the kind of certainty that makes doubt seem like a disease. The purely positive power of this energy is something he can feel inside, it is something he has developed an inner awareness of.

"I believe that you are playing from the heart," said De Roche. "You play with a lot of feelings. I remember one time I was playing in Honolulu, and I got up and I told them, 'I am going to take you guys on this journey for 45 minutes.' I said, 'After each song, don't clap, because I am going to stop and get another flute.' At the beginning, the kids in front were fidgeting and people were looking at their phones. But when you start playing, you can feel the energy from the audience. Then, the kids sitting there are not moving. Minutes after, the MC returned, and it was like the people then woke up. You use your energy as you are playing."

De Roche said that the Native American flute's six-hole primary note scale makes it one of the easiest of all instruments to play.

"It doesn't take a lot of air, either," said De Roche. "I can sit someone down and teach them the scale in 15 minutes."

Ultimately, art has allowed De Roche to find rest in the light, the calm of a lake without ripples, to rise to another plane. Perhaps it's not exaggerated to say that in this case the flute has served as the instrument of divine will.

"During the day, I will sometimes see the flute by my chair, and I will pick it up and play it," said De Roche. "If I didn't have the flute, I wouldn't be around."

Troy Evans

From The Penitentiary to The Big Screen

Troy Evans sat in his cold, compact cell at Montana State Prison mulling his future. Sentenced to 40 years for assault, he had heaps of free time to ponder.

Growing up, he had been a middle-class kid who aspired to become a politician. Decades later, he was now a Vietnam veteran-turned-bar owner-turned-convicted felon ensnared by steel bars, maximum-security cells and courtyards manned at gunpoint, filling his time by writing love letters on behalf of his illiterate cellmate.

Where to go from here?

"There I was, sitting in my prison cell one day," Evans, who grew up in Kalispell, recalled over the summer from his Los Angeles home. "I'd been in Deer Lodge about six months. I knew that I was never going to be governor of Montana or the president now. The military wasn't in my future. I couldn't own a bar any longer, or be a teacher, or be a lawyer. So, I started assessing my options. Where else could a lunatic drunk go?"

The answer, he decided, was Hollywood.

"Nobody minds if an actor has a felony conviction," he said. "So, I ended up in a profession where it doesn't hurt to be a little nuts."

Against the longest of odds, the desperate prison plan proved fruitful. Today, with an acting resume that features more than 50 films—including "Ace Ventura: Pet Detective," "Fear and

Loathing in Las Vegas" and "Demolition Man"—and at least 400 episodes of television to his credit, the former "lunatic drunk" is now a successful character-actor.

From Montana to Vietnam

EVANS WAS BORN in Missoula in 1948. His grandfather, also named Troy Evans, was a state senator from Silver Bow County who served as state boxing commissioner for a couple decades. His father, Leo Bruce Evans, was a World War II fighter pilot who flew more than 30 missions in a North American P-51 Mustang with the 78th Attack Squadron over Japan, including the initial air raid at the Battle of Iwo Jima.

"He was a real, 100 percent war hero, and when he came back, he used the G.I. Bill to launch a business selling and repairing office equipment," Evans said.

The Evans family lived in Ramsay, 10 miles west of Butte, and Missoula before moving to Kalispell when Evans was in first grade, their family swelling to nine children along the way. The Evanses owned a Tasty Freeze on South Main Street in Kalispell and later changed the name to Leo's Lazy Lion, which remained a popular drive-in hamburger stand for years.

Evans' initial love in life was politics. At age 8, he plotted a linear equation of steps that would lead him to become president of the United States. He still had that dream in mind when he graduated from Flathead County High School in 1966 and, later, when he enrolled in classes at the University of Montana. But his trajectory changed dramatically after he was drafted by the U.S. Army in December 1967 and shipped to Vietnam in May 1968 for duty with the 25th Infantry Division.

"I idolized my grandfather and my dad, who were both Republicans, and since they were interested in politics, I was interested in politics," Evans said. "I watched the 1956 Republican National Convention at 8 years old and formed a plan to be the first person in my family to go to college, become an attorney, a state legislator, a governor, a senator, and then to sit in the White House."

After he spent a year crouching in the din, darkness and death of the Vietnamese jungles, however, politics now seemed like a morbid game of deception.

Introduction to Acting and a Life-Altering Night

THE TROY EVANS who returned to Montana in the summer of 1969 was markedly different than the one who had departed for the jungles of Southeast Asia. Fueled by a gut-churning sense of rage, the troubled 21-year-old drank and fought incessantly and cussed venom at his neighbors.

"I was pretty much out of my freakin' mind and mostly unaware of it," he said.

His first job as a reintegrating civilian was at First National Bank in Kalispell, promoting Mastercard charge card accounts.

"The old farmers just kept asking, 'Why wouldn't I just use my own money to buy things?'" Evans said. "The bank president was my girlfriend's father, and he hated my guts because he didn't want me to marry his daughter. We broke up, and I lasted about seven more minutes after that."

One Saturday afternoon in 1970, while enrolled in classes

at Flathead Valley Community College, Evans was "fairly drunk" and standing on Main Street in Kalispell when he was approached by a mustachioed man wearing a white pinstripe suit and a straw sailor hat, with a cigarette flopping in the corner of his mouth. It was Ron Danko, a professor in the English department who was starting a theater and seeking recruits to perform in "The Odd Couple."

"He was not getting an adequate turnout, so he went out on the street and was looking for actors," Evans remembers. "I said, 'I appreciate it, but I'm not an actor.'"

Danko told him he already had a "real actor" but was looking for a "slob"—his Oscar for "The Odd Couple."

Evans accepted the part, a wise decision that would have sterling repercussions down the line.

In the summer of 1970, Evans and a friend converted a large three-story building, formerly an icehouse and more recently a shuttered John Deere dealership, into a diverse if unlikely entertainment hub with a dance hall, bar, art gallery, repertory theater, roller-skating rink, flea market and commons area.

"The walls were three feet thick and filled with sawdust," Evans says.

His next business venture was leasing property near Sykes Diner and opening The Powder Keg bar on July 1, 1971, the day the drinking age was lowered to 18.

"The Powder Keg bar was a riot," he says. "There was no other place close to hear rock and roll for a 100-mile radius. If I hadn't been such a raging alcoholic, there still would be a thriving business there today. It was a dramatic time—Northwest Montana in the '70s ... It was a fantastic, riotous couple of years before I crashed and burned."

Tavern owner wasn't the smartest profession to pursue for the self-described "obstreperous alcoholic," a volatile combi-

nation that came to a head one evening when he addressed a dispute between two patrons by violently attacking the instigator, an assault that left the man with broken legs.

"The move was a U.S. Army heel stomp," he said. "I dragged him out and threw him into the street."

The man turned out to be an attorney. Instead of the "stern lecture and $75 fine" he received after previous bad behavior, this time the "stakes were way higher."

Sentenced to Montana State Prison

After his arrest, Evans committed himself to a VA mental hospital in Sheridan, Wyoming, for 90 days. Sober and hopeful, he and his attorneys believed he would now elude a lengthy prison sentence and be granted another slap-on-the-wrist lease on life.

"I thought that I had beaten the system," Evans says. "I

thought that the time at the VA hospital would show me in a better light and that it would be a six-year suspended sentence."

The judge, however, sentenced him to 40 years at Montana State Prison, with six years suspended. Evans believes the unusually stiff sentence may have been rooted in personal vendetta: the judge had unsuccessfully run for political office in Silver Bow County three times, each time losing to Evans' grandfather.

"It was years before I had learned of the connection that (the judge) had had to my family," Evans said. "The legal system acknowledged that I had gotten screwed. In retrospect, whether he had an ulterior motive or not, he actually saved my life. If the sentence had been suspended, even though I'd been to rehab, I might have gone three or four months and then figured that I could have a beer, and the whole ride would have started all over again. After sending me down to the license plate factory, I decided that I was never going to put myself in the position again where this could happen to me—and that I would never have another drink."

Taking Advantage of Second Chances

BOTHERED BY THE CIRCUMSTANCES of his sentence, the sentencing commission at Montana State Prison kicked Evans loose after two years behind the immense gray sandstone walls in Deer Lodge.

Upon his release in the fall of 1975, Evans enrolled in theater classes at Montana State University. He then followed an ex-girlfriend—the Kalispell banker's daughter—to Berkeley, California, and later drifted to Santa Maria, where he found a summer job working for a community theater company. As it happened, Ron Danko had moved from the Flathead Valley to Salinas, California, and was operating a theater there. Danko encouraged Evans to accept an assignment in the summer of 1976 from a well-respected director in Santa Maria named Donovan Marley. Evans agreed, and worked his way into the local and regional theater scene.

"My entire career has flowed out of that," Evans says.

In 1980, Evans signed with an agent and, one year later, was selected for a minuscule part on the television series "Lou Grant."

"I went on the set of Lou Grant for one day and I had that little scene where I go into the convenience store and I get murdered," he said. "And it was a great experience, except for that I was murdered in the episode. As an actor on a TV series, you never want to be killed."

A few years later, Evans landed a role on "China Beach," which he said was "directly from the connection to the theater in Santa Maria." That later led to his casting as a desk clerk named Frank Martin on the hit "ER," appearing in 129 episodes.

Success as a Character-Actor

INDEED, TROY EVANS has built a vast résumé playing bus drivers, farmers, gunners, military teachers, scoutmasters and, in the most ironic of niches, deputies, sheriffs and police sergeants in a broad array of TV programs and films. He even got a brush with politics by playing a Montana congressman in the HBO series "Veep," and he points out that his role as a Vietnam veteran in "China Beach" was notable.

"Seldom will you see a veteran working on a military show," he said. "When I think about the huge numbers of shows—from 400 TV episodes and between 50 and 60 movies—considering that I was 29 when I started, that's pretty shocking."

Evans might not be an A-list celebrity, but his face is familiar to millions: as Roger Podacter in *Ace Ventura: Pet*

Detective; the basketball coach in *Teen Wolf*; Sheriff Perry in *The Frighteners*; and the tough-talking cop in Sylvester Stallone's science-fiction *Demolition Man*, to name a few. Evans currently portrays a homicide detective nicknamed "Barrel" on the Amazon series "Bosch."

"I've been asked over the years, 'How do you pick your parts?'" he says. "My answer is simple: 'If they will hire me to do it, that's the part that I pick.' It is like a tumbled ball in Bingo: whatever square that's called out and I land on, that's what I'm doing to do. And I have enjoyed it all."

Singer-Songwriter Christy Hays

A Stowaway Texan At Home in Butte

Lately, singer/songwriter Christy Hays admits she's in a funny, in-between place, addressing and confronting the ups and downs of existence.

The big, musical havens where she formerly resided, Nashville and Austin, have gotten too overwhelming Hays says, and have become for her an unending cycle of relentless self-promotion and cutthroat vanities. Dwelling upon too many feelings about the music business and her place and position within it, she recently purchased a house in Uptown Butte. After a great deal of wandering, wrangling, lessons learned and enough angst reoccurring, she says she now craves a sense of place, and she might even stay in the Mining City permanently.

Butte is part of the plot but not the whole story. Hays' story is the familiar one of an artist who has spent a long period culminating their influences and well-worn road experiences into art. She has successfully followed the formula, releasing records, touring, and riding the summits and ditches of the requisite life.

She's an introverted, circumspect woman of Midwestern stock, the daughter of a welder and a nurse who was raised in an agricultural town of about 4,000 in Illinois. While she never aspired to be a working songwriter, she's always held the poet's sense of perspective: reflecting on her first memories of her youth, she described the dramatic shift from small, family farm agriculture to the advent and proliferation of industrial farming. The bitter reality of identity loss imprinted.

"I've always been hyperaware and maybe that's been difficult for me," said Hays. "I feel as if I have a deep, internal sense of justice, in a world that is inherently unjust. It's been a learning process for me over the years to compartmentalize what I don't understand. I'm definitely an escapist and I've lived different sort of lives. I came to Butte and it's not a Utopian thing for me. Butte is strange and messed up and yet it's really awesome."

As a teenager, there was no intrinsic pressure to play music but the energy of it eventually prevailed. She ditched Illinois while in her early twenties and within a few months of graduating college embarked to Alaska. "Disillusioned," she says, by some our society's coarser aspects, she disappeared into the woods.

Song writing and the act of self-dredging ultimately triumphed over her more isolationist instincts. She moved to Nashville in 2007 and after two years relocated again, this time to Austin, Texas, which at first felt "more her speed and her vibe." She expanded her musical repertoire and found a little solace in the city's legendary collaborative spirit.

The past ten years she has worked her medium, delivering quality material, landing radio airtime, and even sharing the stage with other talents such as Sturgill Simpson and Jeffrey Foucault, among others. Hays' singing voice catches like a briar; it doesn't tear its audiences but sticks to them. She plays with precision and without prejudice and without illusion. As a singer-songwriter, she has learned to do it right—and done it. If you want a bit of bittersweet joy from the work of a solid vocalist and lyricist (begin with "Town Underground"), Hays is your girl.

At first, Hays spent a few weeks of summertime in Butte, gigging regionally, writing, and embracing her beloved quietude. While she cherished her relations in Austin, she started to find the sort of mental and material culture there very difficult. And while Nashville, she says, is "way more obsessed with commercial success" than any other place she has lived, Austin's population has ballooned as one of the most explosive growths in the country.

"I don't have that innate drive to live that way anymore," says Hays. "There is solace here (in Butte). The residents are mostly elderly and at the beginning I was treated with distrust: 'What's this lady doing here with her out-of-state plates?'

"Now it has more of a feeling of going home," Hays says of Butte. "I can regroup and not be out on the bar scene or worrying about how successful I could be or won't be. The writing is conducive here. It's an exciting new phase."

From the historian Joseph Kinsey Howard who called the Mining City "the black heart of Montana" to Butte native Berton Braley who wrote, "If you've got red blood in your veins, you'll like her," authors, poets, historians and entertainers have interchangeably complimented and criticized it—sometimes all in the very same paragraph.

Food critic Anthony Bourdain tidily described the hilly territory built on copper, crime, and plenty of contrast: "At first look, you'd think this is the worst place on Earth. A ravaged, toxic, godforsaken hill threatened from above, riddled with darkness from below. But you'd be wrong."

Hays does anything but glamorize Butte or trivialize it, she simply accepts for right now it's a calm and peaceful setting which provides her with the legroom and head space to observe her feelings, perceptions and countless thoughts. She's at a defining point in her relationship with both Butte and her art.

Reevaluating her own notion of self, she has formed a non-profit songwriter and writer-in- residence program called Dear Butte, an artistic retreat for like-minded people who need to get away from the cityscape to create.

Perhaps the peace and happiness of forming Dear Butte means no more yearning—or at least a temporary cessation of obsession—for Hays. Thinking of Hays abbreviating her fine career is unavoidable, yet she is at the crossroads of realizing different needs.

"I am at the point where I am not completely sacrificing or pursuing or obsessing over carving out my own career. That's where Dear Butte came from, the need to live a whole and happy and fulfilled life. Music and notoriety are inherently not fulfilling. To provide the wherewithal and the support and to open up a lot of artistic doors for others, to me, that is exciting."

Skip Horner

Victor, MT

Dashing Explorer Guiding the Continents

Skip Horner knows a sensational or unusually adventurous experience when he sees it.

Not only does he appreciate the spirit of adventure, but he also lives it, breathes it, thinks it, traverses over it, spryly leaps across it—and he makes a living sharing such extremely bold and unique undertakings with others.

For Horner, participating in enlivening and original enterprises—whether it's white-water rafting in Madagascar or Papua, New Guinea; scaling the summit of Mt. Vinson, the tallest peak in Antarctica; or ascending Gunnbjornsfjeld, the highest mountain in the Arctic—isn't just a job, but rather a lifestyle choice that melds together his happiness, personality, and broad knowledge.

Horner explains: "The experience of seeing new foreign cultures and wildlife scenes keeps me going. This curiosity is always there. I'd love to be able to go to every country in the world to see what's happening, but there are way too many places to go. If a year has gone by and I haven't visited a new country or culture, then it hasn't been a good year."

Originally an East Coast guy, Horner moved to Aspen to become "a ski bum" in 1969, a time that he refers to as the town's "golden age." The glitz hadn't taken effect yet, open space was plentiful, and real estate prices weren't so exorbitantly unreasonable. During his second year there, he discovered the fabulous fun of cross-country skiing, even using it

as a mechanism to transport himself back and forth to town, and from the mountain where he'd downhill ski by day to the teepee he called home that winter.

Years later, Horner began teaching cross-country skiing. One day, on his way to work, he noticed a man distributing brochures for a local river expedition company, and after a little bit of schmoozing, Horner had a job guiding folks through the Grand Canyon on the Colorado River.

After three summers and 21 trips guiding the indubitably demanding Colorado River, Horner went looking for a new direction in life. Law school was supposed to be a definite destination, but that never panned out because he got hired by a different adventure travel company named Mountain Travel. This job established the foundation of what would become his life's work.

"At that time, I still thought that guiding was something I could only do before getting serious about life. I was still thinking that it couldn't be a career."

In 1974, Mountain Travel sent Horner off to lead climbing and trekking expeditions to just about everywhere in South

America, as well as throughout the ruggedly remote expanses of the Himalayas. The early 1970s, he says, brought the emergence of the adventure travel industry. Then, the concept of world travel was far more obscure and mysterious, and, unlike today, guidebooks to every single country in the world weren't available at every bookstore and coffeehouse in town.

"Basically, [back then] you would fly into a place and then start asking questions. [Mountain Travel] would send me a plane ticket to almost anywhere—could've been Katmandu or Santiago, Chile, or Nairobi—and I'd pick the client up and take them on a trip."

After leaving Mountain Travel to do his share of solo globetrotting, Horner began offering his own guided services. Starting and maintaining an adventure company, he says, wouldn't have been possible without the inestimable help and the exuberant encouragement of his wife, Elizabeth.

It's been more than three decades since he began experimenting with world travel, yet Horner believes that a good guide doesn't need to have previously visited a country in order to be a competent escort for a client. In fact, he says that if a guide possesses a keen understanding of geography, topography, and cartography, and practices clear, logical thinking, then that person should be able to safely and successfully guide folks through unfamiliar terrain.

"My expertise isn't in having been to a place and therefore knowing everything about it; my expertise is in knowing the patterns of places—how mountains work, how rivers work, and how travel works—so when I get to a new place, I can use this understanding of patterns and systems to make a new trip work. If you can understand the motivations of people, and have compassion for the people whose country you're going to, you'll be fine."

However, such bold and risky undertakings are closely associated with uncertain outcomes and inherent danger, which does alarm Horner. But fear, he says, is a critical emotion necessary for an adventure guide's success: Have it and it can be consciously counteracted to make a trip thrive, or used as an adrenaline boost to prevent things from becoming routine; lose it and things may become uninspiring. Either way, a good guide, he says, doesn't mind sticking his neck out in an unfamiliar place.

"The first time I took people to Mt. Everest, I hadn't been there. Some people like that type of adventure. My fear of falling has made me a successful climber; and as a guide, I'm always afraid of having a disastrous trip. When pulling into any new town, I'm a little bit up on edge, a little bit excited, a little fearful, but you can control this fear and make a success out of it."

After many years of living a life fraught with extreme exquisiteness and dicey endangerment, the single most beautiful, powerful, and emotional thing to ever affect Horner is a solar eclipse. It's an outstanding astronomical event that he's seen in some far-flung places, including once while cross-country skiing through the frostily cold confines of Mongolia, and yet another time when leading a caravan of camels across furrowed sand dunes deep in the Sahara. (Horner is already organizing trips to view the next four solar eclipses from unusual places.)

"A true solar eclipse is the most unbelievable event a person can experience. It's so outrageous, so unbelievable, so moving, that you have to see it for yourself to understand it."

Often Horner passes through and pops up in places so remote that his presence compels some locals to suspiciously scratch their heads; others to wipe their eyes in disbelief, as if they were looking at a mirage; and a few to even fretfully hurry for the hills.

One time, when Horner was guiding a white-water rafting trip in Madagascar, his party pierced through an eerily remote stretch of water and waited on a quiet beach to meet a helicopter. Horner was guiding for an adventure company named Sobek, which at the time was receiving much positive publicity in Madagascar. The helicopter, which was supposed to skirt the group around a singularly treacherous arrangement of waterfalls, was just part of the hullabaloo thought up by an oil company hoping to capitalize on Sobek's newfound publicity.

"We pulled ashore with eight days' worth of scruff and grunge, with our beards and boats and life jackets, and we landed along a village full of kids. They saw us, and as we got closer to them, they ran away. It was very funny for us, because we could see them peeking at us through the brush and bushes."

There, on this distant and far-off beach, an incredible scene took place, with boats arriving, a helicopter landing, and a pair of roaring twin-engine planes circling—all punctuated by groups of animated Westerners in funny dress, including the U.S. ambassador to Madagascar.

"We had a cocktail party right there, and people were looking at us like we were from Mars. Who knows what kind of mythology came out of that day. Can you imagine what kinds of stories have been passed down in that village?" asks Horner, who fell violently ill that same day due to a mosquito bite he'd gotten on a previous trip, the nip incubating into cerebral malaria.

While pockets of relatively uncharted territory still exist in the world—where few people have ever ventured, places so remote that little human interaction transpires there—today's trekking groups will take clients to nearly anywhere on the planet. And chances are that Horner's already blazed those ill-defined trails. In fact, he will visit the same place twice if he really loved his first experience there. And if he keeps finding enthusiastic people who want him to lead them on a trip to a particular place or predicament, he'll repeat such a journey as many times as wished.

Come February, he'll be shepherding an expedition to Mt. Kilimanjaro to summit Africa's highest point for what'll be his 24th time. Even though he's been there and done that many times over, Horner's enthusiasm for this approaching ascent has by no means worn thin.

"I love going with people that are excited, that get something out of the trip. I refer to the people that come with me on these adventures as friends. I see it this way: It's a relationship that's between friends. I'm doing what I love doing most and I'm doing it with my friends. I love taking people to places who desire to understand where they're going, and that's fun no matter how often I've been to a spot."

Even after 30 gripping years in the business and a few close encounters and unnerving brushes with doom—such as when, two years ago, he was buried under an avalanche in the Himalayas and watched with incredulity as thick snow slid, tumbled, and disintegrated before his eyes, all the time thinking he was a goner—Horner, who's the first adventure guide to take clients to all seven continents, scoffs at the very notion of the "r" word: retirement. To him, cozy couches, slow strides, and casual, unhurried living aren't vicissitudes favorable to conducting a life, but mere episodic interludes between absorbing adventures.

"This is my life. My life is my work. For me to retire would mean that I'd have to quit traveling and guiding. I can't do that."

Ericka Kirkpatrick

Twin Bridges, MT

For This Second-Generation Hatter, the Details Matter

As a kid Ericka Kirkpatrick sewed sweatbands inside of cowboy hats and cleaned them with excited alacrity. Traipsing throughout her mother's millinery shop, she would find bags of multicolored feathers intended to be used as inseam and fling them in the air. It wasn't all mischievous; there was also work to be done on the tall sanding machine where she would patiently hand-sand cowboy hats.

Rubbing the gritty paper against the brims wasn't exactly typical child's play, though it kept her smiling and occupied, and it was safe and gradual enough that she couldn't do all that much harm (to either the hat or herself). Even today, the tactility of turning hats—the repetitive feel of how the fibers soften the more you roll them—provides comfort to Ericka, who is now a full-time milliner.

"Sanding hats is a good childhood memory, like having a blanket," said Ericka, the owner of Montana Mad Hatters in Twin Bridges. "It's been my favorite part as an adult hatmaker."

Growing up in landlocked Montana, one of Ericka's earliest childhood ambitions was to work as a marine biologist. That yearning passed, and when she enrolled in a number of communications classes at college, it was in hopes of becoming a news anchor. But she realized quickly that the nervousness she experienced while standing in front of a camera wasn't something she could conquer—and that craving too passed.

Ericka eventually returned to hats, first working under mother, Sheila Kirkpatrick-Massar, a notable hatmaker, who up until a couple of years ago based her business in Twin Bridges. Ericka's plan was to start her own operation where she lived in Wisdom. For a brief time,  mother and daughter worked in two separate locations: Ericka started the hatmaking process and Sheila completed it and fitted all the customers. But after Sheila closed her shop, a series of events yanked Ericka out of Wisdom and pulled her back to Twin Bridges.

At 33, Ericka is combating preconceptions that are both gender-based and generational, finding that most men, especially seniors, have a hard time deferring to a woman, especially to one who appears to be even younger than her age.

"I'm lucky because my mom paved the way," said Ericka. "You prove yourself and prove that you know what you are talking about. I've learned to stand my ground a little more and to be persuasive. "

Perhaps her mother understands the importance of the role of the hat in the cowboy way of life more than most. In fact, she built her first one more than 40 years ago. Her daughter's involvement in the craft wasn't something she had predicted.

"My whole goal as a single parent, raising Ericka, was to buy this building and sell the business with it for retirement, and I never thought that any of the kids wanted to take it over," Sheila said.

In the fall of 2017, Ericka returned to the same building that her mother had shuttered. She hauled in the boxes of old hat fitting blocks and plugged the equipment back in. Her learning curve was admittedly steep.

Ericka felt intimidated by the prospect of having to fill such large boots. After all, Sheila, who was inducted into the Cowgirl Hall of Fame in 1992, had built hats for celebrities and a number of current male hatmakers have learned the fine points of their profession from her. From the start, however, Ericka has been determined to prove that she's not just riding on her mom's coattails. Like that little girl who pitched the feathers in the air, she's parked in her mother's footsteps; yet, she has her own personality and passion.

"I want to make my own mark, my own way, and prove that I can make a good hat. This was not just inherited, but to make it my own."

Business is a challenging world and Sheila is constantly learning on the job. But no matter what is asked of her, there is little at this point that Ericka can't either figure out or improvise, and if she gets into a jam, Sheila lives less than 15 minutes away. Hatmaking is the kind of love that needs testing—and Ericka knows that it is real.

"I've gotten a little more backbone for it than I did before. I don't get quite as intimidated when people come and pick up their hats."

As a matter of fact, Ericka's backbone holds firm enough to ensure the completion of each new task, her overall knowledge of the trade seemingly satisfactory to both client and kin.

"I just had a guy message me the other day," Sheila said. "He said to tell Ericka that he got his hat. He said, 'I love it.' He said, 'it's perfect.' That he tried it out at a wedding. It's awesome. I shared that message with her, and that gives me great pride."

SEAN KOCHEL'S FOLK ART INSTRUMENTS

MISSOULA, MT

THE MERIT OF ORIGINALITY is not trendiness; it is sincerity.

Sincerity is what distinguishes the guitars of Missoula's Sean Kochel from others made from machines or shadowy factory lines.

"They are not cookie-cutter stamped," says Kochel, born and raised in Shelby. "And there is definitely quirkiness to my guitars, because I do make them from my own hands."

Originality is what his customers clamor for.

"The thing that resonates from people who have bought a guitar from me is that, unlike buying a guitar from the music shop, one of mine, they say, feels as if it already has a soul inside of it."

The soul of which is bred with a distinctly Montana tinge.

"I feel as if the guitar helps them to be an even better musician, because it already has a soul and local reclaimed character built into the instrument itself. That is a contrast to a 1972 Fender guitar, which takes decades to find its soul."

Singer-songwriter J.R. Rogers owns several of Kochel's guitars, as well as "a beer can microphone, and a cigar box amp" made by the craftsman.

"Each one seems to have an artistic character and soul that is completely unique and inspiring," says Rogers. "His instruments make me want to play music in different ways than normal rehearsal, therefore, offering a good catalyst for creativity."

In Kochel's universe, innovation is measured in the sum total

of his thoughts. Montana is on his mind—and imparted into his product. It could be a guitar nut made from the boiled down bones of an elk; it could be a guitar neck that traces itself back to an old growth Montana poplar tree; or it could be wood salvaged from an 1860s immigrant-built homesteader barn or an 1890s railroad icehouse.

"To be able to have something that is part of our history—our Montana history—something representing our existence on earth, is something that people connect with."

Kochel guitars are generally built from western larch, fur, or pine trees. Not leaving anything to chance and refusing to be duped by aesthetics, he rigorously tests the wood's integrity.

"The old growth trees are much denser and much more tonal than the trees nowadays. So, if it has a dead sound, I'll rebuild the guitar. If it sounds like a dud, it's out. A lot of times, I will be listening to see if the guitar lends itself to a song. It's like any other experience. You can tell if something is good or bad by going with your gut reaction."

Much of the lone wolf guitar maker's preparation is mental.

"Psychologically, I always try to tell myself how good it is to be doing what I'm doing. I try to keep a positive attitude. I'm always telling myself, 'wow, this is cool. This is awesome. I can't believe I'm in my garage building this guitar.' I need to keep this attitude or else it doesn't work out."

Judging from conversations with some of his clientele, things are working out just fine.

"First off, I love my Kochel guitar," says root-blues hybrid musician Reverend Payton. "I am a bit of a guitar fanatic. I especially love strange and vintage instruments. It is pretty much what I am known for. I have a unique style, and because of that I am very picky regarding instruments. Kochel created a one-of-a-kind instrument for me. The neck is huge, which is just how I like it. It has .243 Winchester shells inlaid into the fret board. It has 12-gauge shells for volume knobs. It is as much folk art as it is an instrument."

"Kochel Guitars are works of art and great instruments," says Luther Dickinson, former lead guitarist of the Black Crowes, now finding success with the North Mississippi All Stars. "The attention to detail and overall aesthetic and sonic quality is instantly appealing and satisfying. Kochel guitars are beautiful, and they rock."

Dickinson discovered one of Kochel's guitars serendipitously—out of thin air, literally.

"The North Mississippi All-Stars did a show in Bozeman," says Kochel. "One of my guitars was hanging on the wall, which I left at a recording studio. At the beginning of the performance, he grabbed it off of the wall and started playing it. He never played it before in his life. He never set it down. I let him have it as a gift."

Both Reverend Payton and J.R. Rogers came across Kochel's guitars on his Etsy site, and Kochel has shipped guitars to all of the seven continents, except for Antarctica.

Kochel recently shifted focus away from cigar box guitars after he recognized an "oversaturation in the market."

"I had to either change or forget about it. I have confidence in my guitars, and I believe I fill a niche in the boutique guitar market. I still stick with my tradition, with all of the wood I use being reclaimed. Ninety percent of the major guitar manufacturers source things out to China to be brought back here. People realize that. They realize their guitar is not made by a man's hands, but from a machine."

Indeed, there are those who support Kochel because they support art and talent that is quirky, eccentric, and provincial, those who admire the designs of a man who in many ways mirrors his birthplace.

"They support me because they know that I'm a Montana guy who is shaping their guitar neck in my shop with a file, and that I'm doing it all by hand in my shop. They know I'm carving the guitar bodies with a chisel. There is no truer sound, and it helps give their music a distinct and unique sound."

Herman Melville once said, "It is better to fail in originality than to succeed in imitation."

Kochel has succeeded in originality because he, admittedly, is too stubborn, too entrenched in his ways to imitate or to follow along on the weak path of compromise.

"I just sent a guitar to Brazil," says Kochel. "I even made a guitar for the number one musician in Botswana. Things are good."

Senior Hiker Mario Locatelli

"The Mountain Goat of the Bitterroots"

PERHAPS WHAT IS MOST FASCINATING about Mario Locatelli isn't what he has achieved, but when he has done it—and first committed to doing it.

Standing a smidgen over five feet, at first glance most wouldn't consider Mario to be capable of accomplishing the list of hiking endeavors that he is credited with. Further inspection of his sturdy calves, or a brisk walk with him up a favorite mountain, will convince anyone that the robust octogenarian has done what he claims.

Much has happened in the eight-plus decades since Locatelli was born near the Italian Alps in Milan, Italy, on December 21, 1932, third in line of what would come to total 12 siblings. He immigrated to the United States, in 1948, with a brother, sister, and two cousins.

He moved to the Bitterroot Valley in 1973, after he, his wife, and daughters were on their way to Yellowstone National Park, and they drove through the Bitterroots and were captured by its scenery: slow-melting snowfields; exquisitely developed rock glaciers; deep green bodies of water; high boulder fields and dense forest.

Two years after that initial awe-inspiring trip, he and his family bought 80 acres near Woodside at the confluence of a spring. He "worked like a jack ass" as a wrecking contractor in Oregon to be able to purchase this land, and considered himself "semi-retired."

One year later, he and his wife of 22 years divorced. A second marriage was even less successful, lasting only briefly. From the ashes of these separations, he found a new purpose. "After my (first) divorce," says Locatelli, "I used to go to the bars a lot and swap stories and hear sad people. I was as unhappy as possible. It didn't take me long to realize that I had to do  something else—something happy, something worth it— with my life. I couldn't just hang out in the bars—too many depressed people with problems."

A short walk turned into a long hike; a brisk day hike turned into an overnight backpacking trip. Then came the boulder-hopping and ridgeline climbing, and, over the years, Locatelli hiked all 39 canyons from Lolo to Nez Perce, covering the entire trail and ridge for each one.

"I truly know my father," recalled daughter Cathy Locatelli. "Over the years I have watched him accomplish feats that cannot be explained of a 140-pound man. Determination, will, and desire are all I can come up with to describe who he is. He has taught me and proven to me that you can't let your mind talk you out of something. If your heart says you can, by the grace of God and your desire, you can. What started it all were the trips to mountains. He was reborn there."

"Mountain Goat Marathon" Race

Soon, Locatelli gained notoriety for the grueling "Mountain Goat Marathon" cross-country races he organized in the Bitterroot Mountains in the late 1980s and early 1990s.

Picking a name for this fundraising event would be easy, after all "Mountain Goat Marathon" did have a nice ring and hard-earned connotation to it. At 6 a.m. on July 15, 1989, the era of the Mountain Goat began. The hike spanned 25 miles, beginning at Twin Lakes, at the head of Lost Horse Creek southwest of Hamilton. Due to the responsibility of organizing this new event, Locatelli didn't participate in the race, instead making certain to count heads and take names. All proceeds from the inaugural race were donated to the Lifeline program at Marcus Daly Memorial Hospital

The route of the 1990 Mountain Goat Marathon covered 25 miles across the rugged wall of the Selway-Bitterroot, beginning at Twin Lakes on the edge of the Idaho border to Hamilton, with elevation variations from 6,500 feet, up and down across the canyon walls to the tallest summit of Ward Mountain,

9,119 feet. Hikers struggled most of the race along elevations of more than 9,000 feet covering most of the same rugged terrain as last year, except now it covered Ward Mountain peak and ended at Roaring Lion Canyon. At the age of 57, Mario won his own race in 7 hours, 40 minutes. The Mountain Goat Marathon course record was eclipsed three years later by 36-year-old Scott Leibenguth, in 6 hours, 59 minutes.

After bagging a few more of the western states' highest points, Locatelli, at age 63, decided to make it his goal to visit the highest points in each of the Lower 48 states. In October of 2003, following eight years' worth of exertion, this High-pointer successfully achieved that goal when he ascended New York's Mt. Marcy.

Oldest Person Climb Mt. McKinley

On July 5, 2003, at 71 years and 6 months, Locatelli became the oldest man on record to summit Alaska's Mount McKinley. (McKinley was later renamed Denali, but both designations are acceptable and interchangeable.) Scaling the 20,320-foot peak completed his mission of reaching the summit of the highest mountains in all 50 states. It took 16 days to reach the summit and climb back down.

Indeed, thin altitude, fierce weather, and active glaciations combine to make Denali one of the most difficult and severe mountains in the world to climb. When you are more than 70 years old, it's ten times more difficult to climb it than it would be if you were 30. Your heart just doesn't beat as fast at that age; oxygen doesn't travel as quickly to the heart, lungs, and brain, and Locatelli's guide, Zach Shlosar, decided that the West Buttress route would be best suited for an older man's fitness and capabilities. Given a Grade II, the West Buttress shares with the Muldrow route the status of having the lowest grade, which implies it is the safest route to the summit, and relative to other climbs on the mountain, it is considered simpler, because the terrain is less tricky. But as Locatelli was warned prior to embarkation by Shlosar: "it is never easy on Denali."

Shlosar, then 33, had been climbing since 1983, and had started guiding on McKinley when he was 18 years old. His personal climbs already included trips to East Germany, the Swiss and French Alps, Patagonia's Cerro Solo, and multiples ascents in Alaska's Tordrillos, Chugach, Talkeetna's, and Denali's Northwest Buttress.

Shlosar carefully picked Locatelli's route for its aesthetic quality and climbing terrain suitability. His expeditions are goal-oriented, with carefully thought-out climbing strategies to the summits, but also focus on the goal of increasing clients—as well as his own—mountaineering skills. He had all the necessary criteria required of a savant shepherd: extensive prior climbing experience, proven physical and mental stamina, and a gutsy attitude. To Shlosar, his treks up to Alaska's highest point had been the final self-exam in a climbing progression that helped him become a strong and capable mountaineer prepared to climb the world's great mountains.

"McKinley is a terrific challenge," said Shlosar. "To climb it at any age is an accomplishment, to do it as old as Mario, even more so. People turn back all the time on McKinley. Some are determined to make it yet can't. Some have the heart, will, toughness, and preparedness to do it, but I've never seen a guy Mario's age, before or after, that had all those qualities."

To celebrate, Locatelli did a headstand on the blustery summit.

Spirit of the Goat

FOR MARIO LOCATELLI the mountains will always keep their mystery—and resultant peacefulness—and their poignancy is still searing. By their sustained giving, the ridgelines and rugged canyons erased his feelings of dislocation and emotional exile and gave urgency to self-transformation.

The Bitterroot Mountains will always hold the spirit of his life. He's one of the lucky ones.

From the time he headed out into the Selway-Bitterroot, in his late 50s, to the time he climbed Mt. McKinley, he saw life as a challenge, as well as a grand adventure in which he needed to play his part fearlessly. Nothing would hold him back, and even when the odd adversity arose, he saw it as part of his learning curve and accepted it with a mischievous grin.

Most of the secrets for longevity that the "Mountain Goat" promotes, well, aren't really secrets at all: exercise strengthens bones, muscles, organs and joints. Without adequate exercise, the body degenerates. As long as you have a body, it needs to be regularly worked.

"I try not to think and talk about getting old," says Locatelli. "I feel young and fit. Most guys in their 50s and 60s, they are just pups now. When I hike up a mountain, some of the guys behind me are half my age. I can still hold up with the best, and that's a good feeling."

At 80 plus, Locatelli is just one of the many super active or super successful doers and thinkers who continue to work and play at peak performance. All could easily have slipped into the physical and emotional retirement malaise years ago, but they forged on—happily.

Scientists have put forward a raft of reasons for these differences over the years, ranging from lifestyle choices, such as smoking, to genes. For Locatelli, the mountains have provided a place of clear thinking.

Hiking has allowed him wander in concentration, to let it all go. For years Locatelli told himself that he wasn't going to carry negatives around; he was no longer going get riled up about them. Whatever pains there may still be, he refused to allow them to alter his peace of mind.

On the rugged slopes of Hamilton, Montana's fittingly named Goat Mountain, many mornings, Locatelli, alone, bearded, with a fulgent pair of blue eyes, can be seen. The hike that he has done more than any over the years is the one leading up and down Goat Mountain. Though a short distance, 1.4 miles, it gains 1,698-feet of vertical. It's certainly a vigorous test for anyone—any age. While the mark he set at Mt. McKinley was erased by an even older skier, Mario has his gaze fixed on setting new ones, including becoming the oldest person to climb Devil's Tower in Wyoming.

"At my age, all I can say is that life is good," says Locatelli.

Rancher-Crooner
Sam Platts

Silver Star, MT

Sam Platts entertains in a style that echoes the familiar lines of traditional country music. As the leader of Sam Platts & the Great Plainsmen, however, he clings to a honky-tonking mode steeped in rustic elements. Lately, not only has he been singing the songs of the country crooner, but he's been living the life of the rancher well.

"I accidentally fell into the ranching career about five years ago," says Sam Platts, a Wyoming native now resident near Silver Star, between White Hall and Twin Bridges.

"I was playing music full-time while living in Pony, in Southwest Montana, a few years ago. But the locals couldn't get their heads around a guy in his 20s, who didn't do anything all week, but who hit the road on the weekends, made music, and who was living on the weekends. The people of Pony and Harrison thought that I should do something more productive with my days and the Jackson Ranch, outside of Harrison, was looking for someone to feed cows for a winter and to help them calve. Ranching is not the most financially fruitful, but it's a satisfying job. I get plenty of material out of the ranching lifestyle."

On this particular evening, Platts has just returned from his day job, feeding cows, carrying out pedestrian ranch chores, finishing whatever tasks need to be done.

"Right now, it is calving season and all of the cows are having babies. Knock on wood we haven't had to pull calves so far this year."

Considering the category of music that Sam chooses to play—a straightforward, non-showy 1950s style of traditional country typified by the prime cuts of Waylon Jennings or Merle Haggard—perhaps it's not too surprising that he ultimately found another occupation as a rancher. Platts grew up in southern Wyoming, where he heard plenty of classic country (and scores of polka jams, too) while driving around on his great-grandmother's ranch alongside his father, Scott.

In addition to ranching, Scott was also a nimble-fingered luthier; Sam had worked at his father's shop, in Saratoga, Wyoming, building stringed instruments. After school, the teenager would spend a few hours laboring at things such as filing frets or sanding guitar bodies. An experienced traveling musician, Scott himself had also gotten plenty of mentorship.

"It wasn't as if I would sit down and have lessons with him. I would go off in my direction and I would get hung up and he was always there to show me where to go…My dad was way into listening to polka on the way to do the haying. My grandmother was into classic country. My dad was in bands for as long as I could remember—and he still is. He played in a band (called Rimrock) in Wyoming for 20 years and he's in one in Washington now (called Bottom Dollar)."

At age 21, Sam answered an advertisement on Craigslist seeking the services of a steel and lead guitar player. Noted

yodeler Wylie Gustafson, of Conrad, Montana, was the posting party in need of a supporting musician and within three
weeks of Sam acing his audition, he was on tour with Wylie &
The Wild West in, of all places, Russia.

It was from Wylie that Sam learned the models of showman-
ship and professionalism, as well as the rhythm, eloquence,
pace, progress, timing, and minimalism of a style of music that
he considered authentic.

"You've got to keep it simple," explains Sam. "It's the less is
more sort of mindset. Like a conversation, there are people who
are quiet and to the point yet come through loud and clear, like
a guitar player like Don Rich or Buck Owens. Being flashy is
not always the right thing to do, especially if you want to have
that good backbone of traditional country western swing, with
good shuffles, and something that's danceable…Songwriting
is like that, too. When you break down a Kostas song, they are
simple, but they are perfect. He could break your heart in three
and a half minutes."

Sam recorded his first independent and wholly original
studio album "Sundown at Noon" under the name Sam Platts
and the Kootenai Three, in 2013. Arrangements mirror the
style of songs that he heard many years ago while he was riding
in the pickup truck on the family ranch. He even added the
accordion—his grandfather's favorite instrument—to parts of
the band's music.

"We started in Idaho in Kootenai County and recorded the
first album at Jereco Studios (in Bozeman) and that eventually led us to moving to Montana in 2014, full-time. My bass
player and I moved to Pony, and we found a place reasonably
priced that had a great small-town atmosphere. We played a
lot of gigs at the Pony Bar. Like most small bars in Montana,
the Pony Bar was very supportive."

Songs in Sam's repertoire range from self-penned originals to the indispensables of time-honored ballads from icons such as Merle, Waylon, and Willie, sounds that perhaps might not mesh well with contemporary country radio. Despite this, Sam says that the music that he values has a beloved, even optimistic, place in his account and vision of the landscape.

"In the last ten years there has been this resurgence of the true honky-tonk sound. People my age—from their 20s through their late 30s—there are a lot of reformed rock and rollers who have been in punk bands and whatnot, and now who have started playing country."

For the past few months, Sam Platts & the Great Plainsmen have been broadcasting a weekly live stream variety show from a rehabbed barn outside Norris. A pivotal piece of the ensemble, Sam's wife, Lilly, is a persuasive fiddler.

"We've got weekly guests and special guests and we put them together like the 60s, 70s variety shows, like Porter Wagoner's or Johnny Cash's. We are the house band, and we have gal singers to give it some variety. About one-third of the show we take up and the guests (which have recently included Kostas and Tessy Lou Williams) take up the rest."

"Right now, I really like the live stream. We are growing our internet following and it's great to play for people that are listening. What started as an idea as how not to slip into obscurity because there were no live songs to sing, has turned into something that we are really proud of."

As it has played out, his love of ranching now contends with his other great affection to play music.

"I work at the ranch seven days a week and I cut out early one day a week to rehearse for the show. Sunday morning, I go check cows and feed cows and then I get out my ranching clothes and do our live stream. This accidental agricultural career has been a big source of inspiration and has gotten me in touch with a different lifestyle, and in touch with the country itself."

DALE ROBERTSON

FORT BENTON, MT

A Legacy in Horseshoes

ART IS FREEDOM to make a choice. Art is making the choice not to satisfy this person or that person, but to be able to make a choice to satisfy your own volition.

At 66, Dale Robertson, of Fort Benton, has made the decision to follow his whims as a horseshoe sculptor.

"I've always wanted to be an artist," said Robertson. "I could've been doing it 40 years ago."

Yet life is certainly what happens as we are making other arrangements, daydreaming about the future, locked in the mental crater of the past. Choice often remains an elusive beast. But it is always the present that dictates—and Robertson's notifies him it is the right time.

Born in Stanford, Montana (population 769, in 2010) Robertson made an effort at agriculture, but times were so lean that he nearly went broke; he recalls a time when his finances were so sparse that he sold cribbage boards of elk bone to hold the imp of poverty at bay. Robertson served in the Navy for four years and after apprenticing under a noted cobbler, he tried his luck at shoe repair.

"I nearly starved fixing shoes," said Robertson. "It was familiar because years earlier, I nearly starved running 1,100 acres of land, which was half wheat, and the other half cows and pigs. It was just too tiny of an operation."

Robertson moved to Fort Benton in 1982 and he eventually took perhaps the most sensible route to solvency, joining the Choteau County Road Department. After retiring in 2015

with 18 years of service to his credit, Robertson revisited the magic space of art and insight.

He started sculpting small metal cowboys, and then he experimented with building furniture, and then after that he tried welding animals of metal pipe scraps. Eventually, he found several well-rusted horseshoes lying on the garage floor. It's funny how a seemingly insurmountable issue such as low self-confidence can evaporate when you show up and try.

"I didn't know I could do it; you don't know it until you try. They may not be as pretty or as perfect as a lot of other people's art, but they are not doing horseshoes. You start with the feet and go up, you build one leg, build the other, connect them, and go back and forth. I've gotten better with practice and I'm getting close to the real deal. I'll run my hand over the metal and if it's a horse sculpture, I have to have it feel like a horse."

In that same garage, Robertson stands adjacent to small buckets and fatter tubs of horseshoes of every degree of tarnish. In one corner, there are barrels of horseshoes donated from a horseshoer in Fairfield. "They are a godsend," said Robertson. "People are hoarding them now as souvenirs or decorations."

Step one is that the majority of the horseshoes need to be stripped of pesky nails. In a crevice below a workbench, they are then sorted into buckets of clean, or nail-free, shoes, which are then tumbled for a couple of hours to shake off the rust. The horseshoes are tossed in a cement mixer with small chunks of gravel, the gravel acts like a polisher.

"I spend hours in here," said Robertson. "I listen to music and go do it. I could spend the whole day here. Except in the summer, it gets too hot, it can be miserable. Who wants to be in the garage? My heart's just not in it. But I am a guy who needs to be busy all of the time."

Robertson's tools are minimal: a two-burner propane forge, a vice to bend metal, a plasma cutter, a wire welder. Minimal is not to be confused with simple or lethargic, as the forge splatters sparks and emits fire.

"There are times when I can feel my shirt getting warmer and warmer," said Robertson. "When you are working with hot horseshoes, you won't forget to put your gloves on."

Robertson's horseshoe sculptures, some of which exceed ten feet in height, require the welding of hundreds of pieces. One moose, darkened with a durable undercoat varnish, required 700 shoes. The delivery of that sculpture to the town of Monarch became, literally, a delicate balancing act.

"I had to drive 45 to keep it from flying off the trailer," said Robertson.

Robertson has an admiration for the welding process, especially the fact that no situation exists that he can't get his artwork out of. Nothing is unbreakable; everything is subject to re-fix.

"With welding, you think you are doing a good job and then you find a spot where you've messed up. You try to fix it sometimes and it gets worse. The fun part is that you grab a big hammer, and it doesn't hurt a thing when you take to it.

I had a sculpture that the hind quarter wasn't right, so I took it back. I can cut them up and start over. I took it back and started over—just needed a cutter and acetylene torch."

Peering into one of the larger installations, one can see the curves and muscles and the action of the animal. Indeed, Robertson is a skillful synthesizer who has created a small legion of inventory to choose from and enjoy.

"Everyone is an artist," said Robertson. "Though, it's a tough field. I see it this way: if I enjoy it and you enjoy it, well, that makes it better."

Robertson generally sticks to the fabrication of bulls and horses, though he talks of expanding into other less conventional forms. "I like cowboy things," said Robertson. "I'm a cowboy. Personally, I'm pretty much an elk and deer kind of guy."

There are several words that Robertson uses frequently in this conversation: choice, freedom, happiness. But there's also desire. The artist in Robertson wants it because he wants it.

"This will be around a long time after I'm gone," said Robertson. "It'll be nice to leave a legacy instead of nothing."

There is something pure, talented, exciting and folksy about Robertson's sculptures; when viewed standing together in the front yard of his home, it's easy to envision the assembly of a folk-art park to be enjoyed for generations. Indeed, many cars already travel down the dusty stretch of road to examine the metal-ring stallions, bears and moose.

"Now if someone drives by, I just sit in the kitchen and I watch them," said Robertson. "I don't go out there, just let them look. There were a couple of times I might have scared them off when I came out. I thought, 'well, that's too bad,' because I just wanted to tell them about them."

BILL RYDER

Metal Artist Welds Scrap into Horses

CREATIVITY IS ALWAYS A LEAP OF FAITH. Writers sit down in front of empty pages. Painters stare before blank easels. Thespians rehearse looking toward empty stages.

Metal artist Bill Ryder's leap of faith is experimental by nature. He explores his creativity with Smith Corona plug-in typewriters, antique Dromann seam machines, silvery cable chains discovered at garage sales, sheet metal from Pacific Steel, and the curved internal organs of 8 mm projectors purchased from thrift shops. His leap of faith is as much self-exploration as it is the celebration of the torch flickers and vintage portions all part of the process.

"You just need to get a whole bunch of stuff together, start making it, be brave, and whack it up," said Bill Ryder, noted primarily for this metal horse sculptures.

In the yard of his Helena home, there are plenty of unique materials waiting to be repurposed into welded metal art: small packages of fixtures picked up at the estate sale of a former plumber; tire chains to eventually be re-used as part of a horse mane; heavy steel bicycle parts, pawn shop rescued tools; Domestic Rotary antique sewing machines.

"I try to stock up on the castoffs," said Ryder. "A lot of this stuff you can get on Sunday half price at estate sales. But if you want the good stuff—like some of the sewing machines—you have to step up. This one cash register down here has so many different pieces, buttons, and great linkages."

Bill's welded metal artistry is a family affair, for he is joined by his wife, Julie, on projects. The pair often place driftwood in the scaffold of his larger horses. Bill collects the driftwood and Julie positions it. Some of their horses are embedded with more reflective items, such as a deceased lineman's belt buckle or military insignias or mementoes.

All Ryder horses begin with steel telegraph wire, copper coated welding rod, or electric fence wire. After the heat of the torch attaches the frame, it can be filled in with various kinds of rusty, vintage ingredients. Sometimes Bill will wrap brass or ceramic around the steel framework of the horse and weld them. No matter what is applied inside or to the exterior, the finished product is handsome, strong, and immortal.

Perhaps the immortality of the work stems from the fact that the Ryders do not believe in the idea of a useless mechanism. In their estimate, there is nothing obsolete about a broken contraption. If a machine no longer clicks or whirs, it is still a beautiful piece of equipment chock-full of complex mechanics. Indeed, old devices provide simple artistic solutions, both the questions and answers.

"Finding a lot of the old beautiful stuff has a lot to do with perseverance," said Bill. "With welding and repurposed art, I can create it as fast as I can think about it. With welding, I just do it. If I don't like it, I can cut a chunk off. It's not pottery or something that you have to wait three weeks for."

During outings to antique stores, junk shops and garage sales, the Ryders discover items that they perceive as all part of a continuum; the artistic force in question is perpetuity, the eternal mode of expression, the deliberation of past, present and future. Typewriter parts receive special consideration.

"I make frequent stops at the thrift stores looking for typewriters," said Bill. "If they are nothing special, like mid-1950s, they are sadly just thrown into the metal recycling."

Bill said that most of the pieces he cannibalizes for parts hold more of an intrinsic value than a financial one. But even if that were the other way around, he said he would still dissect them.

"I picked up this old black typewriter once," said Bill. "And as rare as I thought it was, it was selling for $12 as a collectible on EBay, with free shipping. There are millions of them—old typewriters. So, I just go ahead and use them. They might as well be reborn into something else, something that will stay around."

The son of a mechanic, Bill Ryder's passion took on a decidedly repurposed quality years ago when a momentary respite from the daily grind allowed him to better focus on the medium of sculpture. Torch in hand, auto-darkening helmet clamped around chin, he began creating unique "assemblages" and horses made of inexpensive vintage finds and old unwanted objects. He packed his frames—mostly ones resembling horses, ranging from miniatures to ten feet tall—tight with mechanical density. He raised enough interest to warrant teaching welding and art classes.

Bill chuckled as he recalled a recent welding class he instructed in Lewiston; the class focused on the construction of small-form horses.

"The folks in Lewiston were pretty eager," said Ryder. "It was supposed to be for the basic beginner. You know, really easy and small stuff. You give them options, small things, dead parts and pieces, horseshoes. Some of the folks got really excited, and they started dragging in old car frames and big things."

Bill Ryder is a bit of a freestyle creative entrepreneur. He's a businessman when he has to be. Half the time he has to concentrate on the business end, but generally he is most comfortable when his creativity is at the forefront. Holding a box of wooden white piano keys, Ryder contemplates their future insertion. "I am sure I will find a project for that." He picks up a helical scan reader yanked from the guts of a VHS recorder. "You couldn't create that," he says. "Maybe you could. But it would take a lot of time. I'm going to take it ,and it will become something more when it is put inside of something else."

Originality is the essence of Ryder's veritable scholarship. Creativity is his soul. His degree is in the resurrection of memories and the belief in nostalgia; some of the best things in life are those forgotten trinkets you have to go digging around for in a closet corner or on a sandy shelf in the attic.

"So many of the parts would be part of something that would be ordinarily sitting around collecting dust somewhere," said Bill. "After I get done with them, they are part of a horse—a piece of art—that people can pass on to their kids."

Horse Archer
Pat Stoddard

Conrad, MT

FROM THROWING TOMAHAWKS to chucking spears, to targeted marksmanship with a bow and the dexterous display of swordsmanship—these are just a few of the things that showman Pat Stoddard can do when he is mounted in the saddle.

First and foremost, however, he considers himself a practitioner of horse archery—the centuries-old practice of shooting a bow while on horseback—a devotee committed to teaching its forms.

Stoddard, of Conrad, said that his introduction to horse archery—and the entertaining aspects of horsemanship accompanying it—connects to the early 1990s, and he's been dazzled by both ever since. At that time, he was living in Laramie, Wyoming, and he came upon a group of reenactment battlers called the Laramie River Black Powder Brigade.

"There were a bunch of mountain men and Indians and there was an Indian reenactment camp," said Stoddard. "There were 70 people in the Sioux-Cheyenne camp, 65 in the Cavalry, 10 re-enactors in the Crow camp. I'm not Crow, but I just represented them. It was pure warfare for a week—shooting lightweight bows and great big blunts. We'd ride at each other at a full gallop, and you'd try to nail that sucker as you went by."

A history aficionado since he was elementary school age, Stoddard's interest in horse archery then deepened, and he began studying and training its techniques in earnest. Before long, he heard of a man named Lajos Kassai, a notable Hungarian bowyer and horse archer, and soon he attended one of the European man's clinics, in Iowa.

"In 2001, I went to Hungary and trained with Lajos for about 10 days, and I watched him ride and shoot for 10 or 12 hours straight, switching horses every hour or so. It is a feat that is listed in the Guinness Book of World Records."

Since then, Stoddard has been swallowed by the deep and varied cultural roots of horse archery, a practice with a lengthy history that spans continents, to reveal a pair of the rawest motivations: survival and sustenance.

"The Native Americans in North America got into horse archery to hunt buffalo and hunt game," said Stoddard. "They shot with short bows and were deadly with it, hitting their mark at 60 yards at a full gallop. They'd hunt buffalo on a horseback with a bow or a spear… They had sprinting competitions and played different sports on horseback. Some countries got into it because of warfare. There are Viking horse archers who have been found to be buried with their horses. Mongolians were devastating at shooting backwards at a gallop. The Chinese switched from chariot to horse archery and made it (the art of war) more mobile and deadly. The Japanese still do it for religious ceremonies, to bless a shrine."

Testament to its prevalence in far-flung places, Stoddard was invited in 2011 by the King of Jordan (King Abdullah II) to participate in one of the country's most popular horse archery tournaments.

"There were guards running around the playground of the competition area driving one-ton black Chevy pickup trucks with the M45 Quadmount with .50 caliber machine guns mounted on the back. Being that the King showed up, they wanted to have good security. I sat in the camel-haired tents for shade."

Spanish Mustangs Well-Suited; Calm Horse Ideal

PERHAPS NOT SURPRISINGLY, the largely unheralded half of the horse archery team is the horse, yet the animal is equally or perhaps even more important as the archer. Stoddard said that Spanish Mustangs possess the right attitude and aptitude to serve flawlessly the distinct needs of the rider.

"The Spanish Mustangs are the original Indian ponies, and they are actually a kind of dying breed," said Stoddard. "They weigh only 800 pounds, but Spanish Mustangs can pack 30 percent of their body weight, so they are extremely tough."

Stoddard said that it is exceptionally difficult to develop a well-trained archery horse, even a Spanish Mustang, because of all the coordination and comprehension required of the animal, which could easily become spooked by the jerky, unorthodox movements of the rider and the alarming whiz-zing blast of the archery.

"Horse archery requires the need for the rider to use his right leg, his left leg, steer and stop the horse with his feet, all separate from the bow. Then you need to drop the range of the bow, and to use your legs to control the horse and then shoot the bow. The horse must be trained to maneuver all of this and trained to steer anywhere…A horse can be ruined easily, so I don't share my horse. In Jordan, I picked a medium speed horse, and I was hitting what I wanted, and I shared my horse, and after that, he was the fastest horse there, and I had a hard time hitting my targets after that."

Stoddard, who uses a wide variety of bows, from Mongo-lian, Korean, Hungarian, and Turkish style ones to homemade productions carved from hickory, said that the ideal horse for mounted archery would be one that is level-headed and calm, and perhaps even lazy to some degree.

"Some horses get scared by the snap of the arrow, so the training the horse needs has to be reassuring and consistent. The ideal horse doesn't need to be especially speedy, just temperamental and intuitive enough to be put into a slow lope or certain kind of gallop and stay there, to not speed up. The best horse I've ever had for horse archery, I could put a rope and saddle on him and work cattle all afternoon with nothing on his face. No halter. No bridle."

Martial Arts Skills Applied

BORN AND RAISED in South Dakota, Pat Stoddard grew up around the presence of Shetland ponies, a breed that he emphasizes as not being "a kid's horse," but as a bunch of "mean and tough son of a guns." While high-school age, he shot arrows while on horseback, but he didn't stick with it too long, mostly because he had only a few of them at his disposal, and he quickly tired of retrieving the same few ones over and over.

"I remember always leaning toward reading the Indian stuff at the libraries," said Stoddard, age 69. "There were some Indian graves and an old Trading Post near Frederick, South Dakota, that I've never forgotten. I bounced around from South Dakota to Colorado to Wyoming to Montana."

While living in Colorado, he enrolled in ju-jitsu classes and became transfixed by its focus on the transfer of energy as well as its practical use of applying weaponry. He was never too keen on pursuing belts—he craved knowledge. Around that time, he also developed an interest in nunchucks.

"I've practiced nunchucks religiously for 20 years," said Stoddard. "The nunchucks and the martial arts flowed over to the archery. There was a five-year stretch while I was living in Libby, where in the wintertime, I was shooting about 1,000 arrows every day, and I got to shooting 17 yards in the dark and would still have a pretty good grouping. At one point, standing on the ground, I could shoot 15 arrows in 30 seconds."

Teaching Knowledge, Mental Edge of Horse Archery

For years, Stoddard has blended all of the things that he has learned about horses, archery, and martial arts, and combined them successfully as a competitor and entertainer at a number of events in Montana and elsewhere. While he still harbors the urge to compete, he is buoyed by the prospects of sharing his knowledge and experience with a younger crop of riders.

"I'm not denying the possibility of future competition, but I'm in it for the sake of the art. You've got to be shooting at least an hour a day, to build up muscle and instinct. So much of it is mental: breaking down every action into each part and having to think about each part. In horse archery, there has to be a flow and mental connection with everything. Your mind has to be set right for what I'm trying to teach."

The Perfect Polish of Pipe Maker Mark Tinsky

Wolf Creek, MT

Entrepreneurs are by definition a romantic species, perpetually seeking new challenges, new experiences, and new passions. Once the day-to-day operations of their businesses have fallen into a familiar routine, many grow bored stiff.

Not Mark Tinsky.

The Wolf Creek pipe maker isn't constantly trying to re-imagine his role or reinvigorate his attachment to his work. Each and every day, he finds the thrill and the adventure in his commitment to a beautiful, simple idea: to be good at one thing.

"Pipes are not instant gratification," said Tinsky. "It takes years to learn the right packing, the right pipe, the right draw, choosing the right tobacco. Making a pipe is the same way. I've always wanted to do the best I could in one area—just one—instead of trying to do too many things."

People tend to romanticize their own motivations and histories. They value what matters to them now, and forget what really mattered to them when they started. It's human nature, so it's an easy habit to fall into. Tinsky's motivations haven't deviated since 1978, the year he and friend Curt Rollar founded the American Smoking Pipe Company.

"At that time, the pipe makers were Europeans," said Tinsky, 61. "They were Italian, Danish, German, or English. There was nothing local in the United States. We set out to break that barrier. That, and I grew up in the 1960s era of defiance and rebellion, and I didn't want to just do what my dad did or what I was told. I was a history major, but I didn't want to teach. That was what my dad wanted. I came from that time, and I still have that stubborn streak of independence. That's why Wolf Creek is perfect for me. It doesn't matter what car you drive, because they are all full of mud."

In 1990, Curt left the company to pursue other interests, but Mark continued solo, building a reputation using quality briar from Greece and stem blanks imported from Italy. By offering collectors a wide assortment of models and finishes, his handsome, handmade pipes garnered a niche.

A lesson in Tinsky's pipe making is a lesson in the perfectly polished. Pipe construction's primitive foundation begins with Tinsky presorting and hand selecting usable blocks. Grecian Plateaux briar is used in almost all of his pipes. Caringly aged and at first cured in a carefully controlled environment, only the finest briar blocks are chosen. The right slab yields a considerable quantity of straight grains. Tinsky visually inspects each chunk and immediately disqualifies many of them because of their flaws, holes, cracks, veins or because he notices other indicators of future problems. As clean as he would like a piece to be, however, he admits that he can't know what mysteries a particular chunk of wood holds until he starts drilling and cutting it.

"They can't all be perfect straight grains or they wouldn't be worth anything," said Tinsky. "Briar is soft and deep, and I look for a block that fits the shape."

Tinsky said that lines are a predictor of success. Lines are drawn to be followed, followed by his drills and his metal lathes, which chisel out the air hole and tenon hole, and ensure proper depth. All lines must be straight.

"The engineering of a pipe is pretty important," said Tinsky.

"It's like how the foundation of a house has to be straight. My theory of pipe construction is that like in seventh grade shop class, everything starts as a cylinder.

The process allows Tinsky to "make decisions" along the way. Constantly illuminating every nook and cranny eliminates mystery, though his curiosity and the potential for surprise holds firm.

"You are constantly making micro-calculations as to spots or stains, and you are always calculating what to do, checking lengths and angles. With these small calculations you make touches you are not going to get on a machine-made pipe."

One of the decisions that Tinsky frequently makes is to abandon a piece. He generates boxes of rejects and unfinished work, perhaps as many as 10% of the projects end up derailed due to flaws in the briar. Sometimes it's an embedded rock or too much dirt, other times the inside is cracking with sap.

"Pipes don't have to be symmetrical; they can be as irregular as you want. But if the shank is cockeyed, it can't be fixed."

Handmade pipes such as the ones made by Tinsky are a tiny fraction of the pipe market, "probably one or two percent," said Tinsky.

"I guess there is a bit of pipe snobbery," added Tinsky, pipe in mouth, tobacco burning, talking while sandblasting for straight, deep, regulated graining. "But I don't get involved in that. The people I talk to are ones who share my values."

Indeed, Tinsky's clients respect that the pipe maker puts his heart and scar tissue into the product and that the finished pipe instills a sense of struggle rewarded and sacrifice shared. Tinsky's flying sawdust, 2,500 pounds of briar bags, sea of drills, tools, buffers, and ubiquitous tools encourage an organic, intimate experience. This pocket of romantic experience also gives his pipes their uniqueness.

As the sun sinks and the snow swirls and the wind hums against the windows, Tinsky stands in front of a scorching space heater bleached with sawdust. The walls and floors are busy with sawdust. His hands are busy with sawdust. Lastly, he embeds maple wood into a stem for ornamentation and stains a finished pipe.

"Some of the pipes are natural—no stain," said Tinsky. "Others, a little stain is needed to bring out the grain even more. There are dark stains, light stains and more intricate ones. I guess it's all about survival of the cutest, right? The cute cat. The cute kid. It's what gets the most attention. People like beauty."

Tinsky understands that his pipes are not for everyone—he considers his prices "mid-range," as many clients are fly-fishing pipe smokers with decent incomes—and that the default state of the consumer is mass-produced, inexpensive, and impersonal.

"You can go to the drugstore or to Wal-Mart and get a mass-produced pipe for $20. If it lasts that is great or if it doesn't, you throw it away. Similarly, you can buy a piece of pottery or a cup from China. My philosophy is to make a great pipe, show what I can do, and let people make their own choices and decisions from there."

Clancy UFO Library
Tied to High-Profile
Roswell Mystery

On or around July 1, 1947, something reportedly crashed in the Corona, New Mexico desert. After word of the wreckage circulated, Major Jesse A. Marcel, an air force intelligence officer for the 509th Bomb Group, stationed at Roswell Army Air Field, and two Counter Intelligence Corps agents surveyed the area. Marcel later claimed to have found an "aluminum foil-thin metal" that was "indestructible in the debris field," comprising the outer body of the object. Marcel insisted that slivers of metal at the site had "a strange purple writing" on them.

When Jesse Marcel Jr., was eleven, he said that his life took a "strange" and "wondrous" turn late one summer night in the kitchen of his family's modest home in Roswell, New Mexico. It was there, he said, his father showed the young boy and his mother "the debris from a mysterious crash" that had occurred a few weeks earlier on a ranch approximately seventy-five miles northwest of Roswell.

For the rest of his life, Marcel claimed that his father woke him up in the middle of the night to look at it, telling him it was something he would never see again.

"Though my father was the senior intelligence officer on a base that was home to the country's most closely guarded secrets," wrote Marcel Jr., in his book *The Roswell Legacy*, "he was, to his family, a pretty laid-back guy...But on that night, I saw another side of him. It was a mixture of excitement and confusion, suffused with a sense of wonder that one just doesn't see in many grown men."

Marcel Jr professed that his father had spread across the floor materials and objects "clearly like nothing that had been seen on Earth before."

After an initial report that a flying saucer had been recovered on a ranch near Roswell, the military issued a statement saying the debris was from a weather balloon.

On July 8, 1947 a public information officer at Roswell Army Air Field declared that they had recovered the remains of a "flying disc." By the end of the day, Air Force base commanders released a second press release asserting the material in the debris field came from a downed weather balloon. General Ramey Roger told the press it was "just a radar deflector from a weather balloon."

The item that Marcel Jr., said fascinated him the most was a small beam with purple-hued hieroglyphics on it. Marcel maintained that he and his father were told to keep quiet about what he had seen that night.

In April 1979, Marcel Jr., said that he decided to break his silence, writing to a magazine with additional information about what he had witnessed at age 11.

"Imprinted along the edge of some of the beam remnants, there were hieroglyphic-type characters. I recently questioned my father about this, and he recalled seeing these characters also, and even described them as being a pink or purplish-pink color. Egyptian hieroglyphics would be a close visual description of the characters, except that I don't think there were any animal figures present, as there are in true Egyptian hiero-glyphics."

Interest in the case was recharged, however, when the physicist and UFO researcher Stanton Friedman spoke to Marcel Jr., in the late 1970s.

Friedman wrote the forward to Marcel Junior's 2007 book *The Roswell Legacy* and described him as a courageous man who "set a standard for honesty and decency and telling the truth."

"His legacy is that he had the courage to speak out when he didn't have to about handling wreckage that his dad brought home," Friedman said at the time of Marcel Junior's death in 2013. "He worked with artists to come up with what the symbols on the wreckage looked like. He didn't have to do that. He could have kept his mouth shut. A lot of people did."

Much of the pro-UFO and pro-conspiracy Roswell viewpoint hinges on the value of the Marcel senior's revelations and the belief rested upon his personal stature and reliability. (He died in 1986 at age 79.) Friedman asserts in his book *Crash at Corona* that Marcel "was exactly who he claimed to be" and as such "was an important cog in a machine whose bare outline was just starting to take form. Others claim that Marcel made "self-contradictory and inflated assertions," about not only the description of the debris but his own background

"Marcel said that he had a college degree, was a World War II pilot who had received five air medals for shooting down enemy planes, and had himself been shot down—that were proved untrue by his own service file," wrote author Kal Korff. Korff stated that Marcel was guilty of "exaggerating things and repeatedly trying to 'write himself' into the history books."

Jesse Marcel Jr earned his own dose of notoriety as the son of the man who said he handled debris from the 1947 crash of an unidentified flying object near Roswell, New Mexico.

For 35 plus years Marcel appeared on TV shows, documentaries and radio shows, was interviewed for magazine articles and books and traveled the world lecturing about his experiences in Roswell. He joined the military and later settled in Helena, Montana, where he worked as an ear, nose, and threat specialist. Following the U.S. invasion of Iraq in March 2003, Marcel requested to be reactivated for active duty to serve as a flight surgeon with the 189th Attack Helicopter Battalion, based at Fort Harrison. He died at the age of 76, found dead at his home, less than two months after making his last trip to Roswell. He had been reading a book about UFOs.

Richard O'Connor, Executive Director of the Jesse A. Marcel Library (JAML), worked as an anesthesiologist alongside Marcel Jr., He dedicated the library to father and son and started Crop Circles Research Foundation, Inc., which is "dedicated to increasing our understanding of the UFO and Crop Circle phenomena."

"He was credible," said O'Connor. "I knew him personally. He wasn't lying about what his father brought home. He never embellished, only told what he saw.

"A father and his son courageously came forward to tell the world an important truth. That truth was that the debris they had personally inspected, taken from the site of a crashed extraterrestrial UFO discovered outside of Roswell, was not of this world."

The JAML is nothing like a visit to your standard library, the expression of ideas and free thought are encouraged. Personal UFO experiences may be shared in a non-judgmental environment.

The JAML is located in Clancy, Montana. Its meetings are open to the public.

Reggie Watts

A Great Falls-made, self-proclaimed 'weirdo' is revolutionizing improv comedy

If John Hughes ever directed a movie in Montana, comedian and musician Reggie Watts would've been the star.

Now an entertainer of late-night television recognition, Watts grew up and went to high school in Great Falls, an experience rich with the angst-ridden, coming-of-age plot that Hughes based his 1980s American teen movies on.

"It was like *Sixteen Candles* or *Weird Science* or *Ferris Bueller's Day Off* or *Better Off Dead,*" said Watts, who penetrated deeper into the pop realm as the Emmys DJ in the fall of 2021. "I feel lucky that those movies were around during that time. I was the exact perfect age when those things came out. I didn't stand a chance."

Watts said that he had no trouble finding the rich moments of insight and painful moments of irony in Hughes' eloquent vignettes, and to this day such films resonate in self-effacing, reverent memories.

"I appreciate some of the characters, because I was definitely sort of a class clown," Watts said. "With Great Falls, people either hate it or love it, for sure." Watts loved the northern Montana city for a lot of reasons; it's where he grew up, where he became Reggie Watts, he said.

"While it doesn't have an obvious artistic culture, it was the perfect time to be there in junior high and high school. Dope music. Listening to weird music on boomboxes and playing records, always riffing all the time. It was the '70s and '80s, and you didn't need to worry about cell phones. Good, fun, outdoor activities, like the Boy Scouts. Great Falls allowed me the chance to be who I wanted to be—a weirdo—and there was no bullying, and I met a lot of other weirdos, and we had a weirdo club, which did art, dreamt, did music and had free rein."

Watts said that he overcame self-doubt and the more disorienting moments of his high school years by sampling everything, from participating in sports and band, as well as the drama team and student government, to astronomy and back lawn stargazing, and even a little bit of modeling.

"I wanted to experience as much I could—it's a bad habit," he said.

Watts was born in 1972 in Stuttgart, Germany; his mother is French, and his father was a U.S. Air Force officer. Watts arrived in Great Falls at age 4, and at 18, the 1990 Great Falls High School graduate moved to Seattle and played in bands—punk rock bands, heavy metal groups, you name it—while attending the Art Institute of Seattle before landing in New York in 2004.

"It was a blast to discover being a young adult…and I lived in the classic living-in-a-band house."

Watts' free-wheeling personality can be seen on network television Mondays through Fridays as the bandleader on "The Late Late Show with James Corden," who took over the CBS program in 2017 from Craig Ferguson. "The Late Late Show" is filmed several afternoons per week at CBS Television City in Hollywood.

His appeal is mostly one of personality: He's perhaps the most unrequited, unequivocal face in all of late-night television. Familiarity is another part of Watt's appeal. In a rapidly changing world, he's something solid, something people can rely on.

Watts plays a jocular, easygoing part on the show, the equivalent to Paul Shaffer, sidekick and musical leader for the entire run of both David Letterman's "Late Night" and "Late Shows." The secret to Watts' success isn't elaborate at all: he's himself.

"James [Corden] was shown a video of mine from a friend of his," Watts said. "They were looking for a band, a bandleader, a musician type of dude. He said, 'let's talk to that guy.' We had coffee in Beverly Hills. Same thing when I went on [to open nightly] on the Conan [O'Brien] show. It was YouTube videos that did it."

Watts maintains a busy schedule of entertaining as a musician-comedian-beatboxer, known for his sets that he says are pulled out of thin air. Using only his voice and looping peddles, he interlaces music with a monologue of extended metaphors and one-liners and chameleon-like mood shifts.

A set of Watts' looped, layered beats resemble a tasty trip across the radio dial, a jumble of melodies and anti-melodies, with his tender, tough voice sizzling a soul-drenched, hip-hop-pop infusion. Minute by minute, he adds droll wordplay and random lyrics like a new suit of clothes; toss in a bit of free association standup comedy, a sly twinkle, and a bunch of startlingly quick and kooky observations, and you've got a night with Reggie.

Indeed, Watts is the first to concede that if it doesn't sound strange than it doesn't sound like Reggie: his brilliant, idiosyncratic, wandering-around-the-beat phrasing, his distinctive rhythm, the sideways pivots in his arrangements. None of them are developed beforehand. And all that exists are great moments told and sung straight. Indeed, the future of improvisational comedy just might be in real good hands.

"I started riffing learning classical piano at about age 11," Watts said. "It was hard for me to learn pieces completely, so when I got frustrated with it, I'd just riff and improvise. Creating my own pieces in piano class, I became interested in just riffing."

He almost always adds a gig or two in Montana to his performance load, and he returns to visit his mother in Great Falls, a tough-minded place that still supplies him with plenty of grit, affection, and emotional oomph.

"Great Falls is blue-collar and gritty and rock-and-roll, and I dig it," Watts said. "Great Falls is a simplistic stereotype, and I keep it to the people who can appreciate it for what it is. It was a fun, open place for me to develop my imagination. I did my thing there and eventually it worked out."

INDEX

About the Author

Brian D'Ambrosio is a prolific writer of non-fiction and author of several books. As a freelancer, he has a glowing soft spot and warm affinity for enchanting eccentrics. He was nominated for numerous awards for *Warrior in the Ring* in 2014. He lives in Helena, Montana. He may be reached at dambrosiobrian@hotmail.com